The 5 S
of Connection
to Your
Business Brilliance

Master your mindset to take your
business from stormy to successful

Leanne Kabat

Ali, you have been + always
will be my shining light.
I wish you endless
summer days.
Leanne
xoxo

The 5 Seasons of Connection To Your Business Brilliance: Master Your Mindset to Take Your Business From Stormy to Successful by Leanne Kabat.

ISBN Number: 978-1-7335410-0-8
Cover design by NewBreed.Design
Interior design by Ekow Addai
Published by Leanne Kabat Media
Printed by Gorham Printing, Centralia WA, USA

For current content and event info,
please visit www.5SeasonsLife.com

The 5 Seasons
of Connection
to Your
Business Brilliance

Also by Leanne Kabat

The 5 Seasons of Connection to Your Child

The 5 Seasons of Connection to Your
Child: Parent Companion Guide

Contents

Setting the Scene

W*e'd just moved our* family from Ottawa, Canada to Seattle and we were settling into our new life. My husband was away on a business trip when one night I cuddled in bed with Alex, 4, and Nicole, 2. Being almost five months pregnant, I happily fell asleep with them.

During the night, got up to use the bathroom but as soon as I stood up, I blacked out. When I came to, I couldn't move. At all. I was paralyzed on the floor. Through a tiny slit in my eyes, I could see the bedside clock. 2:00 am. Then it was 3:00 am. 4:00 am. I started to panic. My kids are asleep right there. I fell on the baby. For hours, I negotiated, demanded, and then begged the Universe to let me move.

Around 7:00 am, a burning sensation erupted in me and everything started to spin, but I could move. I cleaned up, woke my kids, and we rushed to the hospital to check on the baby— thankfully he was unharmed. The brain crash wasn't a one-and-done, though, and most days, I was dizzy, confused, agitated, and experiencing terrible pain. After my son was born, both the testing and the symptoms increased.

Finally, in November, eight months after the first incident, my doctor said she didn't know why I had the crash, why I slurred, saw pink neon flashes shooting across my eyes, or had crushing head pain. What she knew, however, was that it was going to kill me. She said, "Go home, hug your kids, put things in order. With what we see, you've got five years to live."

That next year, every medication and treatment I tried left me weaker and sicker. After three more years, I'd become a shell of a person and a completely disconnected mother. Those were the darkest times.

Then one day, someone close to me reassured me she would step in to raise my kids when I was gone. *Um, what? I was their mom. I was supposed to raise them. Me. No one else.* That was my tipping point. Screw my illness, screw the doctors, screw their stupid death date. I went for a walk, crying and cussing, and decided I was going to fight to live, no matter what.

I plunged deeply into self-care: sleeping when my kids slept, eating brain-building foods, hiking among the trees, practicing deep gratitude and prayer every day. I neglected housework and stopped pretending to have it all together. I simplified our life to focus on one fun thing every day. I reframed my five year expiration to into a fun life goal—vowing to visit fifty countries before I turned fifty, a huge stretch at the time!

One day at the school pick-up line, a mom offered me tickets to an event she wasn't using. I politely declined, but in my mind I screamed, "I don't go to events, I don't do things. I'm dying. Any day. Any minute. Any second." She insisted and put two tickets for a new mom conference in my hand.

That day, as soon as I entered the hotel, the air was electric. We heard inspiring speakers and had deep conversations about love, loss, parenting, guilt, freedom, burden, and joy. I'd never been around women who revealed how hard life could be juggling everything we do: our spouses, kids, parents, pets, the family schedule, vacations, bills, housework, toned bodies and homecooked meals. I thought it was just hard for me, but everyone felt the same. I loved the power of us being authentic and vulnerable together.

After the event, I emailed the conference organizers and told them if they ever needed help, I would gladly volunteer. The next year, I jumped in and a long-neglected professional spark was ignited in me.

During a 2013 checkup, my neurologist showed me my latest brain scan. Our routine was for her to show me the progression of brain damage, and I would fall into despair. But this time, I challenged her. I said the scans didn't measure my passion for making a difference, they didn't show how I woke up every day full of love for my family, how much I wanted to make a difference. I went on and on until I noticed her wiping away tears. She said, "Leanne, you're my miracle." I shook my head and replied. "No, I'm just living in *my* miracle."

After years of helping host this conference, I had the privilege to buy it. MamaCon was now mine! I held multiple events a year for years, and every single day I was thrilled to have such a meaningful, heart-centered business. Yet I tortured myself with negative thinking, panic, doubt, worry, anxiety, and stress. Who was I anyways? Those years were stormy times for me.

Then one quiet morning, God gifted me with a revelation- a smart, solid way to do things better in my life. Ideas flooded me and could barely keep up. From the second my pen touched paper, I was outlining the 5 Seasons philosophy. Right away, I knew this was something that would change my life. I had to share it.

I wrote *The 5 Seasons of Connection to Your Child* with the hope of helping parents nurture deeper, more meaningful interactions with their kids because being connected to others is the key to happiness, growth and love. Curiously, after the moms mastered the 5 Seasons with their kids, they asked me to teach them how to use the 5 Seasons to get through the dark and stormy times in their small businesses. Because of the high cost of childcare, non-existent support networks, and other complicated logistics, I discovered most moms weren't returning to their careers. They wanted to find new ways to contribute financially, but on their terms, on their time, while being present for their kids. This book is for these ambitious, dynamic, magnificent entrepreneurs and entrepreneurs-to-be.

As you read *The 5 Seasons of Connection to Your Business Brilliance*, select the strategies that make a difference right away, and save the rest for later. Modify everything; there's no one-size-fits-all solution! We unlock our business brilliance when we recognize the different seasons and learn how to harness them to be our best. There will still be cool, Fall days, and even Winter storms, but with this framework, I know you can lead your powerful, confident, capable, determined entrepreneurial self through the rebirth of Spring towards long, beautiful Summer days.

Sending xoxoxo's for your journey,
Leanne

EXPLORE. DREAM. CREATE. WORK

BELIEVE IN YOU

MAKE TIME. MAKE GOALS. MAKE MISTAKES.

TRUST YOUR INSTINCTS

GET IT DONE WITH FOCUS & GRIT

BUILD YOUR DAY ON WHAT IS MOST IMPORTANT

SUCCESS IS AN INSIDE JOB

BE
RELENTLESS IN PURSUIT OF YOUR DREAMS
RELENTLESS IN PURSUIT OF YOUR PASSIONS
RELENTLESS IN PURSUIT OF YOUR GOALS

HARNESS YOUR 5 SEASONS

CHALLENGES ARE CHANCES TO GROW

POWER UP YOUR POSITIVITY

YOU HAVE ENOUGH TIME. BREATHE.

BRILLIANCE LIVES IN YOU. SHINE ON!

CHANGE WHAT YOU CAN. ACCEPT WHAT YOU CAN'T.

YOU ARE READY

LIVE YOUR DREAM. WORK YOUR PASSION

CHAPTER 1

Seasons in Business

When snow starts to fall and the wind howls through the barren trees, we put on our puffy jackets and trade our sneakers for snow boots. A beautiful summer day means we slip on a dress, slather on sunscreen, and move through the world with a smile. We know what a typical day in each season brings, which helps us prepare for the day.

But what happens when a cold-snap hits in the middle of our lovely summer?

Or a heat wave in the peak of winter?

Every day, thousands of us start our day feeling strong and empowered only to feel deflated by lunch. Or perhaps it seems like no matter how hard we work from sun-up to sun-down, we feel like we're walking through quicksand, going nowhere but down.

Welcome to the world of the entrepreneur, the solopreneur, or the owner of a small business.

Just as nature has its seasons, so does your business. Being an entrepreneur means you will endure the full range of experiences: one day you're creating, partnering, networking, selling, and celebrating. The next day you feel overwhelmed, stupid, unworthy, stuck, or frustrated and your business starts swirling in chaos. Dark and stormy moments happen quickly!

Whatever season you're in right now, you're not alone! As an entrepreneur and coach, I've seen the nooks and crannies of all seasons in both product-based and service-based businesses. No one is immune. Whether your mindset needs a few tweaks, or you find yourself grappling with intense swings between struggle-success-struggle-success, this book will provide a powerful framework to help you have a solid plan to weather every season in your business. With the right mindset, you can more easily attain growth and prosperity in your work life.

What is mindset? *Mindset* is your unique collection of ideas, opinions, attitudes, thoughts, and beliefs about everything in your life and the world around you. Your mindset impacts your habits and behaviors, as well as guides your decisions and outcomes.

The 5 Seasons of Connection to Your Business Brilliance goes deep into your mindset, right to those crucial play-by-play conversations you have with yourself in the dark corners of your mind, when you either pick yourself up or shut yourself down.

The 5 Seasons is not just a book, it's a philosophy.

It's about deciding we want to be more confident and take courageous action every day, committing to achieving our biggest dreams, and doing what it takes to be more bold, brave and slightly badass in our pursuit of those dreams. But the truth is, we often feel afraid, anxious, inadequate, unqualified, or full of doubt. And that fear can stop us before we even start, or pop up to sabotage us along the way.

The time of fear ruling your life is over.

The time of living a 'fine' life is over.

We get one precious life.

We need to create a life that sends us soaring.

We can't wait until we feel ready.

We will never feel ready.

We have to decide we're ready now.

Still not sure? No problem! The 5 Seasons is designed to show us how ready we really are by revealing, layer by layer, our unique business brilliance. Will being a brilliant business owner always be rainbows and butterflies? Ha! Nope. We will continuously experience all five seasons: the amazing, the devastating, and everything in between. But when you learn this philosophy, you will know how to harness the power of each season to be your best, to shine your brightest, and to share your brilliance with the world.

Let's get started!

The Business Seasons

There's a long view of seasons, or business cycles, entrepreneurs experience to varying degrees:

- New idea sparks the start of a business (Spring)
- Secure first clients, taste of success (Summer)
- Business slows. Face stress/doubt/fear (Fall)
- No sales. Feel defeated, a failure (Winter)
- Make a change and secure new clients (Spring)

Some people can set their business plan in action and go with the flow, riding the business waves like a champion. That was not me. At the beginning, I felt every high and every low, giving myself whiplash some days. Have you ever felt that? Maybe you're flying high from having a great conversation at a networking event, only to feel shut down later that day after a lost sale, or feel elated when someone signs up for a free discovery call with you only to feel gutted when you pop onto social media and read about someone else closing a string of high-ticket sales.

We're challenged to live our full experience—which includes the highs and the lows—while being surrounded by other people's public-facing highlight reels. It can push us to question our worth, our ability, and our potential.

The 5 Seasons of Connection to Your Business Brilliance is designed to help you move from stormy to successful using an easy-to-remember system of seasons to identify where you are and where you want to go in your business. No matter where you are on your entrepreneurial journey, this book can help you.

Right now, some of us:

- Have great success in sales but our backend systems are a hot mess.
- Have beautiful color-coded systems but can't pick up the phone to contact prospective clients.
- Have no clue why anyone would buy from us. We believe we have no real qualifications or expertise.
- Hop from shiny object to shiny object, completely morphing our businesses as trends change.
- Are so riddled with stress about competition and the lack of customers we can't see straight.
- Don't really know what we're selling or what problems we solve, but we're busy all day long.
- Can't launch anything until it's totally perfect.

- Are winging it every damn day, praying no one peeks behind the curtain to see we're 'frauds.'

I have never heard of any entrepreneur anywhere who doesn't face some level of resistance in their own mind. Looking deep at your stories, limiting beliefs, and personal baggage is uncomfortable on a good day, and on other days it may even unleash your raging inner critic and you just don't want to go there.

Many people feel their stress and struggle is evidence that they can't do it, they don't have what it takes, or they should stop now. Why? Because it wasn't supposed to be so relentless, demanding, expensive, and so damn *hard*.

How Long Did Confidence Last?

When I purchased MamaCon a few years ago, it felt like a perfect fit for me. I couldn't believe I was so blessed to own my own lifestyle conference for moms!

The first few weeks of owning my own business was a pure delight. I was so proud to say that I was an *entrepreneur*, that I was going to share my wisdom and my passion, making a difference and making money doing what I loved.

Those were sweet, sweet days.

The brutal reality of owning a business came quickly when I needed to navigate the banking set up, licensing, business registration, mileage tracking, website, insurance, contracts, and creating a re-launch plan. All of that came before I even touched what I would sell or how I would cover my costs. Within hours, I was lost, confused, and overwhelmed.

Having a degenerative brain condition forced me to give myself permission to ask the 'dumb' questions, the obvious ones, over and over. But, at some point, I felt beyond saving, even when so many were offering advice and consultations.

Too many times over the first year, I sobbed into the arms of the Universe, or sometimes strangers at networking meetings, begging for a reason why I needed to jump into a 'business storm' by buying an existing entity that I didn't fully understand. I didn't know how to do all the things. I didn't even know what all the things were! I was dropping balls left, right and center, proving I was the worst juggler ever. Through my ugly cries, I begged to know why I didn't have an 'easier' business.

I've spoken with hundreds of women, and many men, and it turns out that owning a business, any business, is not easy, and not one business in the world can make you immune to fear, doubt, and anxiety over your worth and worthiness. You can have a franchise, buy an existing business, or start something from scratch—we're all in the same boat when it comes to our fears and doubts.

When you feel unqualified, unworthy, or inadequate, it isn't about what you're offering, it isn't about who you are or what you're capable of, it's about what you perceive about yourself. Those feelings of inadequacy don't highlight your shortcomings, they highlight your fears. And, it turns out the feelings of being discovered as an imposter, or someone who doesn't deserve any level of success, is not just for entrepreneurs. It applies to anyone doing anything—no one is immune.

Let's take a look at a few others you may have heard of who have suffered from mindset blocks:

"I am not a writer. I've been fooling myself and other people."

— John Steinbeck, American Author and winner of the Nobel Prize in Literature

"The beauty of the impostor syndrome is you vacillate between extreme egomania and a complete feeling of: 'I'm a fraud! Oh God, they're on to me! I'm a fraud!'"

— Tina Fey, Actor, Writer, Comedian, and winner of many Emmy and Golden Globe Awards

"So, I have to admit that today, even 12 years after graduation [from Harvard], I'm still insecure about my own worthiness. Today, I feel much like I did when I came to Harvard Yard as a freshman in 1999 . . . I felt like there had been some mistake—that I wasn't smart enough to be in this company and that every time I opened my mouth I would have to prove I wasn't just a dumb actress."

— Natalie Portman, Actor, Producer, Academy Award and Golden Globe Winner, Harvard graduate. In her Harvard Commencement 2015

"Even though I had sold 70 million albums, there I was feeling like, 'I'm no good at this.'"
— *Jennifer Lopez, Singer, Actor, Dancer, Producer. Lopez is regarded as the most influential Latin performer in the United States*

"The impostor fears had a greater impact on me early in my career. As I entered corporate America, I faced many unknowns. Being a woman of color in business at a time when very few women were in positions of power, I had to learn by trial and error how I was supposed to perform. This made me so afraid of being wrong or 'looking dumb' that I stayed quiet in meetings. I wanted to make sure everything I said was perfect before I would chance saying anything, and often found myself hearing a guy saying what I had been thinking but was too afraid to say. I did learn fairly early on that my being quiet and not voicing opinions only served to create doubts in the minds of others about my abilities."
— *Joyce Roche, President of Girls Incorporated. Board director for AT&T, Anheuser-Busch Co., and Tupperware Corp.*

As we see, struggling with these feelings are not reserved for solopreneurs alone; it's a common condition we all share. Some of us feel it deeper than others, and some of us feel it longer, but we all feel it.

Wouldn't it be amazing to find the magic key to unlock our success and soar to the highest heights once and for all? Sure, but that's not reality. The reality is we need to first understand our current mindset and decide where we want to go so we can get there. You didn't end up here overnight, and you won't get there overnight. It's a process.

This process is different for every single person, making it even more challenging for those who hire coaches or find mentors or take classes to discover the secret to success. The path is not straight and narrow.

Over the years, I've read stacks of business and mindset books and talked to hundreds of women about how to be a successful entrepreneur. Business rules aren't set in stone and there isn't a one-size-fits-all guidebook. What works for one person may not work for another, and what one person does to find success isn't what someone else can copy and paste into their life. How one coach coaches, how one dog groomer grooms, how one builder builds, and how one designer designs is unique to each person. You can't duplicate success for anyone who wants it.

When asked about what it took to be successful, some people said focus on marketing, some said sales. Some said hire everything out, some said do it all yourself. Some said invest in web pages, some said websites are dead and social media is the place to be. Some said only do things that make you money, some said follow your passion and the money will come.

What to make of all this?

There isn't one right answer to anything. There isn't one way. There are only next best steps based on the current conditions of so many things—especially our state of mind.

For me, my state of mind was a hot mess. I worked hard to overcome the many obstacles I had created in the shadows of my thoughts. I needed to rewrite the stories I created to stop myself before I often started! Once I figured this out, I wasn't even playing the same game anymore. I had connected my gifts to my truths and my unique value, allowing me to master a few of my bigger mindset blocks. And, since you're here with me, I can imagine you'd like this for you, too.

> *"I refuse to be the girl who didn't pursue her passions because she didn't have enough belief in herself."*
>
> *~ Author Unknown*

The 5 Seasons of Connection to Your Business Brilliance rewrites the process by challenging some of the biggest barriers to our success, breaking them down into easy-to-understand, bite-sized bits, and then creating new pathways to our destination.

What dream destination is on your business map?

Is it a certain number of clients?

A certain level of income?

A certain level of public validation?

A certain level of freedom?

What is success to you?

What do you really want?

Big questions, I know! Don't worry, we'll come back to those after we dive into the 5 Seasons framework.

> *"Step out of the history that is holding you back.*
> *Step into the new story you are willing to create."*
>
> ~ *Oprah Winfrey*

The 5 Seasons of Connection

I first tailored the 5 Seasons framework to help parents on their parenting journey in the book *The 5 Seasons of Connection to Your Child,* but right away, I realized the framework could help me in dozens of other ways, especially as an entrepreneur.

When someone liked my post, or shared my video, or bought a ticket to my event, the dopamine hit of validation and worthiness always elated me.

In contrast, if I announced an event and no one bought a ticket, or I posted an engaging question on social media and no one responded, my feelings of shame, not-good-enough-ness, and inadequacy soared.

The good times were like long, beautiful summer days, and then some freak storm would blow through my business and I was left out in the cold, dark night.

As I thought about summer days, winter storms, spring thaws, and the chill of fall, I saw astonishing parallels. My business followed the same cycles as nature not just over time, but day to day, hour by hour!

Before I explain this more, I have two disclaimers.

First, I use the word *failure*, especially in the Winter portion of this book, because that's our language, it's how we (entrepreneurs) talk to ourselves. We use *failure* when something didn't go as planned or something didn't meet our expectations. We often tie the word *failure* to *fault*, like, "I failed to meet my goal and it's my fault. I'm a failure."

I don't use the word *failure* to describe your creations, your effort, your performance, your results, or *you* at all! I'm using it because it lives in our own minds. We have taken the word and made it dirty, something to be ashamed of and hidden away. We hide our failures and pretend they never happened.

Posts that don't overperform are deleted.

Courses that don't blow up are removed.

Events that don't sell out are humiliating.

NOPE! NOPE! NOPE!

The root meaning of the word *failure* evolved from many languages and civilizations, but one common meaning is *to stumble.* Nowhere does failure mean *'to fall into a dark hole of despair where everything is lost and worthless and must be hidden in shame.'*

I'm not going to lie, I felt failure was to be avoided at all costs. I had to work hard to shift my mindset to see that failure is not the end of anything, but actually the beginning. "Hmmm. That didn't work. Let's try this!" "Oh, that was an interesting experiment. Look at what I learned! What would happen if I did this? Let me change this thing and try again."

> *"My dad encouraged us to fail. Growing up, he would ask us what we failed at that week. If we didn't have something, he would be disappointed. It changed my mindset at an early age that*

failure is not the outcome, failure is not trying.
Don't be afraid to fail."
~ Sara Blakely, Billionaire founder of Spanx

In this book, when I say *failure*, it's **not** what I believe about you, it's simply how we speak to ourselves and so it may sound familiar to you. (But we will change that by the end, I promise!)

"We need to accept that we won't always make
the right decisions, that we'll screw up royally
sometimes, understanding that failure is not the
opposite of success, it's a part of success."
~ Arianna Huffington,
Editor-in-chief, Huffington Post

Second disclaimer: Four different and distinct seasons don't exist everywhere in the world. If you live along the equatorial belt or close to one of the poles, you may only have two seasons. It's okay. You don't have to live in a four-season climate to get this framework. In the *5 Seasons of Connection*, I use the concept of four seasons symbolically to illustrate the ever-changing relationship we have with our mindset.

Here's a quick overview:

Winter
Winter occurs when we're disconnected from our gifts, passions, and strengths.

In Winter, we feel anger, shame, rejection, disappointment, or unworthiness. This season can break our spirits and stop us from following our hearts and desire. It freezes us into inaction.

Spending the least amount of time here is the goal, but we won't eliminate Winter completely because even our darkest days serve a purpose to show us what we no longer want or what we'll no longer tolerate. Winter nudges us to make way for new ideas, new business habits, new systems, or new creations.

Spring

This is the time to Spring Clean our internal and external systems and structures, giving us the tools and strategies to leave Winter behind. These could be tools we turn to over and over, or they could be something we use once.

Summer

Summer is all about feeling confident, capable, and connected to both our purpose and our impact.

This is the season we want to spend the most time in while creating great offerings, solving problems for our clients, and building our network and expertise. In Summer, our world is bright, our confidence is strong, and we feel unstoppable in our growth and success. Summer isn't about a fake state of perfection. It's a time when you're your best self while doing your best work in your business brilliance. In Summer, you know your worth and your value, and you know that someone's life is better because of you.

Fall

Fall happens when something cold rushes in—a harsh review, an unsatisfied customer, a snarky rejection, or a door unexpectedly or harshly closing.

When we're in Fall, we might see these events as evidence of our unworthiness or our inability to do things right. In Fall, we wonder if Summer was just a fluke, or a lucky break, and that our current negative situation is the true reflection of our lack of ability or our low worth. (Spoiler alert: Fall is lying to you.)

Crossroads

The fifth season isn't found in the seasonal calendar but lives in the *5 Seasons of Connection* model. It's called the Crossroads.

The Oxford dictionary defines *crossroad* as: *An intersection of two or more roads. A point at which a crucial decision must be made that will have far-reaching consequences.*

We make a crucial decision at every Crossroad. Do we turn on ourselves with anger or frustration, which takes us to Winter? Or do we lean into our fears with love and grace and bring ourselves back to Summer?

Owning a business provides us with endless opportunities to stand at the Crossroads. We either choose connection to our truest selves or we choose disconnection.

Did you notice that magical word? We *choose*.

You might say, 'No way, I would never *choose* disconnection! I would never *choose* to destroy my feelings of self-worth purposefully.'

Well, let's explore that.

Choosing Disconnection

We choose disconnection every time we:

- Deny ourselves our desires.
- Go into people-pleasing mode.
- Say *no* when we want to say *yes.*
- Say *yes* when we want to say *no.*
- Tolerate disrespectful behaviors.
- Sacrifice our value to earn money.
- Deny our real feelings in a situation.
- Do things we really don't want to do.
- Put on a mask to hide our true selves.
- Do something we know is wrong for us.
- Suck it up when someone crosses the line.
- Turn a blind eye to a client's opposing values.

There are limitless ways we choose disconnection.

It often creeps in slowly and chips away at us until we look up and think, "How the hell did we get here?"

Antonella experienced this when she disconnected from her business brilliance.

She owns a studio space where she teaches yoga, and when she's not using it, she rents it out to others.

Antonella had great relationships with her providers, but she needed one more to help with her costs. Georgina was a dominant personality, a powerhouse. After two short chats, and going against her gut, Antonella agreed to rent to Georgina because she needed the money.

Georgina signed the standard contract all the providers signed. In that moment, Antonella paused, but dismissed her hesitation and signed it too. Right away, Georgina interpreted the contract liberally and pushed Antonella to provide more services. Antonella, being a lifelong people-pleaser, complied in the name of good customer service. Georgina snapped when the front door mat was not brushed out every afternoon, demanded premium soap for the washroom because her clients expected better products, and she insisted the studio have silent heaters because the current ones were too loud. Antonella came in one day and found a note on her desk saying the floors needed to be mopped every afternoon so Georgina's clients could have the cleanest surface for their practice.

Antonella felt trapped by all the requests Georgina made and was running ragged in her own dream business. However, she knew Georgina was active on social media and didn't want to risk negative publicity. She bought new heaters and hand soap, swept the mat and mopped every day, even coming in on days she wasn't scheduled to go to work.

You wouldn't know she was in Winter, though, because in her interactions with Georgina, she was bend-over-backwards accommodating and kept a smile on her face, behaving as if everything was great. Secretly, her stomach twisted in knots and she was short-tempered with others in her life.

When one provider left, Antonella posted the opening on the staff bulletin board in the office. Georgina fumed that the notice was posted on a day she wasn't working, giving others an advantage. She demanded she receive the open slot. "You're trying to sabotage my business growth!" Georgina said.

Antonella cursed herself every day, calling herself pathetic for putting up with Georgina, calling herself stupid for cutting her precious time with her kids short so she could go mop on her days off, and calling herself weak for not standing up and putting firm boundaries in place.

In our session, I asked Antonella to imagine *I* was Antonella, the owner of a beautiful studio space that provided incredible opportunities for self-care, self-discovery, and self-improvement. She smiled and sat calmly in her chair. I smiled back, then said, "Now I want you to call me pathetic, stupid and weak."

Her smile vanished. She couldn't do it. She couldn't call me those things so we became curious about why she could call *herself* those things, why she chose disconnection from her own business brilliance through her words. It was a deep journey into her 5 Seasons, and it changed her life and her business.

Choosing differently isn't a gift granted to the enlightened few, or those who are flawless. Whether we're seasoned entrepreneurs or new to the business world, we can learn how to bring more confidence and compassion into our self-talk conversations using the 5 Seasons framework.

Now let's talk about the individual seasons, and how *you* can choose to navigate them and reach your highest business brilliance.

CHAPTER 2

Winter

Have you ever stood outside in the deepest part of winter, in the darkest time of the night, and listened?

Winter has its own heartbeat.

There are no birds singing or bugs buzzing like in summer, and there aren't any leaves crackling like in fall. Winter winds howl through leafless trees and it's harsh: cold temperatures, bone-chilling winds, early darkness, and the fewest hours of daylight.

I explain Winter first because this is when most entrepreneurs are hurting the deepest. We feel powerless, isolated and overwhelmed. We're emotionally frozen, enduring the darkest times.

A heaviness fills the air. Maybe even dread.

Bitter self-talk and hurtful whispers are mumbled and muffled, hanging in the air like our frosty breath.

What is Winter?

Just like winter looks different around the world, Winter in *The 5 Seasons of Connection* is different in various business stages (if you're just starting out versus if you've been a long-time entrepreneur).

In Winter, we may feel:

- Unworthy
- Uninspired
- Angry
- Self-doubt
- Self-sabotage
- Apathy
- Procrastination
- Self-blame
- Numbed out
- Disengaged

- Indecisive
- Negative
- Guilt or regret
- Uncertainty
- Social isolation
- Shame
- Depression
- Perfectionistic
- Stress
- Anxiety

When we're in Winter, during our harshest emotional storms, we swear up and down that what we feel is accurate and very real. We say we're failures, that we can't do it, that we aren't _____ enough to get it right, and in these stormy times, we believe our stories because we're just so afraid. To make Winter more intense, our fears can show up alone, or bundled with other fears to really knock us down.

The Deepest Fears that Winter Highlights:
- Fear of rejection (they won't want me)
- Fear of judgment (what'll they think?)
- Fear of failure (I just can't do it)
- Fear of success (who am I to succeed?)
- Fear of surpassing others (I'm such a show-off)
- Trying to satisfy everyone (people pleaser)
- Indecisiveness (I don't want to screw up)

- Comparison-itis (everyone else is better)
- Perfectionism (you must be perfect)
- Burn-out (can't stop, won't stop)
- Hoarding control (it's about trust)
- Feeling mom-guilt/dad-guilt (oh the guilt!)
- Superwoman Syndrome (I *have* to do it all)
- Firestarter (we unconsciously start fires to fix)
- Shiny Object Syndrome (jumping from new thing to new thing searching for *theeee thing*)
- Heavy-hearted (having no fun in a long time)

If you have long-standing low beliefs about your value, worthiness, importance, or relevance, you've likely mastered the 'illusion mask,' where your outward-facing self is what you think the world expects: happy, in-control, totally capable, and detached-enough-to-be-cool. But it isn't your true self.

Even if we manage to smile for our clients, partners, or vendors, we'll secretly blame and shame ourselves for any issues, making our Winter even longer and more intense. Winter is the darkness that consumes our thoughts and says to us, "Yes, I suck. Yes, everyone else is better than me."

These are just some of the dark places we go when Winter arrives in our lives. Unfortunately, it isn't a matter of dark versus light. It goes much deeper.

Scientists have been testing how thoughts influence our thinking, acting, and behaving using tools from polygraphs (lie detector tests) to the most advanced MRI machines. The evidence is clear: every time you have a thought, any thought, your brain releases chemicals.

If you think positive thoughts, your brain releases one kind of chemical. It causes your muscles to relax, your heartbeat to slow down, and your body feels the flood of your happy hormones. You become primed to have a positive outlook.

Guess what happens when you have negative thoughts? Your amazing brain releases a different chemical, a stress hormone, which causes your blood pressure to rise, then your heartbeat races, muscles tense, hands sweat. You may feel dizzy or lightheaded.

You don't have to do anything for either of these physical outcomes to happen . . . you just need to have thoughts! Since every thought is a coded message telling your brain what chemical to release, instructing your whole body how to respond, you can see the incredible power of your thoughts!

When your brain releases either chemical, based on your positive or negative thought, it sends an electric transmission along with it. Think of it like your thought is pasta, and each electric transmission of a thought is one strand of spaghetti. One negative thought equals one spaghetti noodle.

Now, imagine all is good until a customer posts a harsh review online about your slow delivery. If you beat yourself up with negative thoughts like, "I suck. I can't do anything right. Of course, I screwed up," then you're adding a few strands of spaghetti to your bowl.

A few pieces of spaghetti won't fill up your bowl, but what if you repeat that negative self-talk all day long about a hundred different things What would your bowl look like after a week? A month? A year? Bring on the wheelbarrows because you just can't carry that much spaghetti.

Neurons that fire together, wire together.
~ Author Unknown.
Common Neuroscience Expression

In your brain, you actually have long, noodle-like electrical connections. Every negative thought you have will strengthen the electrical connection (like adding a few more strands of spaghetti) to that specific neuropathway. That path will thicken and become more substantial in your brain -literally changing your brain!

When your brain changes, your body changes. We know our thoughts impact our heart rate, breathing, and muscle tension. Did you know that your thoughts also set off a chain-reaction for things like negative changes to weight, sleep, mood, immunity, focus, and food cravings? From our thoughts!

So, how do *your* thoughts impact *you*?

What Brings You to Winter?

Let's think about a time when you were consumed by negative thoughts or self-talk. Try to recall how it started, continued, and ended in your mind.

Most likely, you'll recall all the ways something outside of yourself pushed you into your dark place: a negative review, a harsh or confrontational interaction with a vendor, being rejected by a prospective client after a sales pitch. Now, think about what came *before* you unleashed a Winter storm in your mind by using the questions below as your guide.

Did you decide to try something new?

Did you take a risk you hadn't taken before?

Did you ask for payment instead of a trade?

Did you set or raise your prices?

Did you step out a little further than before?

Did you turn up your inner light a bit brighter?

Any of these can activate your fear-response because Winter won't paralyze you if you just sit there. Still. Forever.

As an entrepreneur, you're likely craving creation, connection, growth, success, freedom, or expansion. You can't just sit there. Still. Forever.

So, you move. Sometimes a little, sometimes a lot. When you do something new, WHAM! Your negative thoughts pounce on you like a starving lioness on her prey, waiting for the perfect, vulnerable time.

Just like physical winter is a time of deeper darkness, Winter with our negative thoughts is a time of deep emotional darkness. It's here where we face the hardest parts of being an entrepreneur—regulating our own responses and fears, quieting the negative self-talk in the heat of the moment, and recognizing our part in any situation.

The truth is, we don't come to the entrepreneurial life with a blank slate. We arrive with:

- Years of hearing, *"You're not smart enough/pretty enough/qualified enough/hardworking enough/ deserving enough,"* to succeed.

- Periods of stress as we navigated our personal, academic, and professional stumbles and failures, enduring judgment/criticism from our parents, teachers, coaches, friends, employers or strangers.
- A lifetime of receiving messages from the media about what success looks like, what a CEO/high-earner looks like, which may not resemble what you see when you look in the mirror.

Without question, we come to our businesses with baggage and memories—both joyous and miserable. We may have created our business from a place of joy or a place of pain. We come with triggers and coping mechanisms in the face of stress, rejection, anxiety, or fear. Intense emotions can be unexpectedly unleashed in moments where our worth is called into question.

In these Winter moments, we come face to face with our cold, dark, stormy *limiting beliefs.*

> *"Our beliefs are like unquestioned commands, telling us how things are, what's possible and impossible and what we can and cannot do. They shape every action, every thought and every feeling that we experience."*
>
> *~ Tony Robbins,*
> *Author and Motivational Speaker*

What are Limiting Beliefs?

Do you ever have the feeling you aren't reaching your full potential? That there is greatness inside of you but some invisible force is holding you back?

What if that invisible force is *you*?

Beliefs are opinions, or *personal truths,* we have developed to understand how the world works. Limiting beliefs do just that- they constrain or limit us in some way. And they can operate in stealth mode, secretly working in the background of our mind, holding us back, down and out for a long time.

Do any of these phrases sound familiar?

- I'm not destined for real, meaningful success.
- Someone else has already thought of this.
- Other people can do it better than me.
- I didn't work hard enough on this.
- I don't have the right education.
- I'm not a *real* businessperson.
- I'm really not that creative.
- I'm not an expert at all.
- I'll never compete.
- I don't deserve it.
- I've failed before.
- I'll sound stupid.
- I can't because . . .
- Who do I think I am?
- I don't have what it takes.
- I'm not tech-savvy enough.
- Entrepreneurs are so pushy.
- I don't know the right people.

- I'm not lucky enough to make it.
- The economy is terrible right now.
- If I ask for help, it shows I'm dumb.
- My stupid idea isn't that great anyways.
- I'm too old/too young/too... anything else.

If you've said any of these to yourself, or if you secretly think they're true, you're not alone.

Most of us secretly keep a huge list of self-shaming statements. What are some of the cruel, critical, destructive things you say to put *you* back in place?

_____

_____

_____

_____

_____

It's not our fault, my caring entrepreneur. We weren't born wearing signs that read things like: *Failure. Loser. Disorganized slob. Little-miss-know-it-all, Pushy-control-freak,* or *World's Worst Salesperson.*

Long ago, someone or something planted these fear-based seeds in our hearts, possibly about totally different things. Over the years, we've held onto these lies and directly or indirectly supported their growth. We think they're a part of us. We call them our personal truths. We think they *are* us.

They are not.

Our fears do many things for us, like help us be more alert when we drive on a rainy night or warn us when there is someone following us too closely. The purpose of fear is to protect us from harm.

As an entrepreneur, our fear works relentlessly against us, keeping us still, stuck, and anxious. We're afraid to stretch or try new things. Entrepreneurs already face constant uncertainty, rejection, risk, and vulnerability every time we do anything in our businesses. When our fears are activated, every change is a danger, every idea is a potential hazard.

One of our biggest, scariest, most paralyzing fears is this: even if we have the courage to go for it and be who we really are, what will others say? What will they say when we fail? Or even when we succeed?

We're social creatures craving social connections. In his book called *Social*, author Matthew Lieberman found our need to connect is as fundamental as our need for other basic human requirements like food and water. It becomes obvious how much Winter we'll endure in order to *not* rock the boat or shake the tree or do anything to open ourselves up to judgement, criticism, or banishment from our peers.

Our fear mechanism, then, keeps us exactly where we just were—no further, no different. That fear becomes our meanest inner critic, our fiercest protector, and our noisiest detractor from being the best entrepreneur we could be. It's fear doing its job.

You might think that you alone have a monster critic inside you. In a way, you'd be right. It's actually a seven-headed monster.

Psychotherapists Jay Earley and Bonnie Weiss outline seven main inner critic archetypes. Our history, upbringing, experiences, culture and religion all influence which of these we acquire throughout our lives, and in what intensity, determining which of these are the most protective, and which have become our own personal kryptonite.

Their seven archetypes are listed below.

1. *The Perfectionist*

   She demands perfection and her demands for results and performance are high. She tells you no matter what you do, it isn't good enough.

2. *Inner Controller*

   She quickly shuts down any impulsive/radical behavior that puts you in danger or risk. She is harsh and shaming when you slip up.

3. *Taskmaster*

   She relentlessly pushes you to rise above mediocrity at any cost. She fuels workaholism.

4. *Underminer*

   She undermines your self-confidence to retain the status quo, protecting you from becoming too visible. With her you feel worthless.

5. *Destroyer*

   She makes pervasive attacks on your core self-worth, shames you, says you shouldn't exist.

6. *Guilt-Tripper*

   She attacks you for a specific action you've either taken/ not taken in the past. She'll never forgive you, and never lets you forget.

7. *Molder*

   She pushes you to fit into a set mold stemming from your family history, culture, or religion. If you go beyond the mold, you'll feel inadequate.

Your mission, should you choose to accept it (which you do because you're still reading this awesome book on how to do it!) is to first acknowledge we all have inner critics, then to bravely face them. We know they are in us, but to really uncover our business brilliance, we must develop ways to keep following our burning passions even when our critics are screaming the loudest.

Your hopes and dreams for your business and your life exist on the other side of fear, but oftentimes our dreams feel soft and fuzzy, a little undetermined or unclear, so it's easy to ignore them, deny them, push them aside, or put them on hold. Fear, on the other hand, is loud and powerful and mean and fast. Like, super-fast. You could just *think* about maybe trying something and BOOM, one of your seven inner critic archetypes unleashes a massive Winter blizzard to shut that idea down immediately. Let me ask you, when do you unleash your worst self-criticisms? When do you have your darkest Winter days?

Most likely it's when you're doing something new, unique, different, or experimental. Your heart, soul and passion want to stretch and reach your full potential, but your fear is thinking, "What's the quickest way to shut this idea down?" Fear doesn't mess around, it goes right for your weakest point.

Every day, entrepreneurs face an invisible tug-of-war inside of ourselves. It swings between our limiting beliefs and our unlimited potential.

Although most business owners start their companies with every intention of succeeding, some saddle themselves with so many limiting beliefs that they self-sabotage. When something doesn't work, they use the negative experience to support their deeply-held limiting belief that they can't be successful. Sometimes they become angry with things outside their control, and sometimes they unleash a Winter storm onto themselves.

The first stage to understanding our darkness is to first make sense of our anger.

> *"For every minute you are angry, you lose sixty seconds of happiness."*
>
> ~ *Ralph Waldo Emerson,*
> *Philosopher, Poet*

The Myth of Anger

Winter often creates swirls of anger, which is a powerful and yet frequently misunderstood emotion. The emotion of anger is blamed for our negative feelings and behaviors, particularly when expressed in a destructive or aggressive way. However, anger is a normal part of being human and is important to our experiences. It acts as an internal alarm and signals that something isn't right.

When you find yourself becoming angry, catch yourself and instead, think about the root cause. Anger is often the mask that covers up deeper feelings, also called *core hurts*, like fear, pain, shame, rejection, powerlessness, or injustice. Using tried-and-true anger management techniques, like journaling your feelings, participating in talk therapy, or meditating, you can safely explore your emotions to dig deeper into the root cause. Ask yourself these questions:

1. Using very descriptive words, what do I feel?
2. What core hurt might my anger be masking?
3. Is there anything in my control I can change?

We often call our emotions 'anger,' but in fact, what we're feeling is frustration or powerlessness. It's this emotion that taps into our fears the quickest and deepest, unleashing our anger response in a given situation. As an entrepreneur, you will have many opportunities to practice how you handle frustration because our businesses test us.

Over and over and over.

In the same old ways.

In brand new ways.

In ways that rob our sanity and leave us stressed.

In ways that push relentlessly towards the edge.

If we can learn to sit with our frustration a little longer before slipping into anger, and even master frustration, we're able to master everything else. How well do you know your auto-response to frustration?

Your Beliefs About Frustration

Answer these questions:

- How do you handle differences or challenges?
- In a crisis, what's your first response?
- Do you ever resort to silent treatments?
- Do you delegate issues for others to handle?
- Do you play blame-games to find fault?
- Do you have to win every argument?
- Do you *give in* to reach a place of peace?

Your life experiences will influence your business journey and impact your behavior in challenging times because we instinctually go back to what we know when we're in fight-flight-freeze mode. If you grew up in a home with conflict, it's likely when you face conflict as an entrepreneur you may unconsciously rely on your same coping mechanisms with your clients, either overcompensating to make them happy, or hiding and hoping the issue will go away.

Even if you had a calm childhood, you may have faced conflict at school, in sports, or at a job which left you frustrated or angry. In every interaction, you collected an inventory of responses to uncomfortable situations – some healthy, some not so much. Most of us learned how to put on a good face outwardly, but it isn't our outward expression that shuts down our business brilliance. It's what goes on *inside* our minds.

ANTs in Winter

In Winter, we suffocate under the weight of our own negative thoughts. Sometimes we respond consciously and intentionally.

Most times, however, we operate under the power of ANTs. Not little creepy crawly bugs, but Automatic Negative Thoughts (ANTs).

Dr. Daniel Amen, psychiatrist, brain disorder specialist and author, coined the term in his book *Change Your Brain, Change Your Life*. He refers to those gloomy, negative thoughts that take us into our deepest days of Winter.

As he notes, one ant at a picnic is fine, just as one negative thought is fine. Hundreds of ants are terrible for a picnic, and hundreds of ANTS are terrible for your outlook on your business or your life. Amen identifies nine types of negative thoughts that poison our brains and destroy our positive outlook :

1. **"Always" or "never" thinking:** this creates polar extremes without middle ground.

2. **Focusing on the negative:** when we inflate the negatives, dismiss or ignore the positives.

3. **Fortune Telling:** this is when we predict the worst possible outcome in a situation.

4. **Mind Reading:** Brené Brown calls these the stories we form without all the facts.

5. **Thinking With Your Feelings:** we believe our feelings without testing their credibility.

6. **Guilt Beatings:** this is layering guilt on our to-do tasks, making them a *should do/must do*.

7. **Labeling:** negative labeling categorizes people, keeping them stuck with that label.

8. **Personalizing:** when it's all about us. If a sale fails, we must've done something wrong.

9. **Blaming:** this is either blaming *someone* or *something* else. We stay in victim mode.

There may be others, for sure, but these are the main responses that most people experience when they are in Winter. Sadly, thinking and believing these thoughts creates a self-fulfilling cycle: when you have these ANTs, you repeat the many reasons you can't succeed. You then collect evidence that supports the fact you can't succeed, so you do less, which means you won't succeed.

As entrepreneurs, we can experience these thoughts at any time, especially when we stretch out of our comfort zone and cause our muscles to tighten and pull. However, it's in these times of stretching that our ANTs scream at us to go back to our original position.

So, what sets off our ANTs?

When we *do* something, *create* something, *try* something, *build* something, *share* something, *sell* something, *buy* something . . . you get the idea.

Why don't we do everything in our power to shut down our ANTs? Well, that's a bit more interesting.

Anger not only creates an emotional reaction (stress, anxiety, tunnel-vision, or spotlighting), and a physical reaction (heart rate races, blood pressure rises), but according to renowned anger expert and author Dr. Steven Stosny, anger also creates a chemical reaction in our body. When we feel anger, our brain secretes norepinephrine, which acts as an analgesic, or a natural pain reliever and numbing agent. So, we experience anger and then immediately we experience pain relief and numbing, which explains one reason why people can remain in a negative relationship with their automatic negative thoughts for years.

Our response mechanisms erupt when we enter a place of fear, of the unknown, of the new. I've met with many business owners who felt powerless and paralyzed when someone or something pushed hot buttons they didn't even know they had.

Hot Buttons

Hot buttons are issues that are emotionally charged, and can incite our ANTs right away, such as:

- Making mistakes (feeling inadequate)
- Not knowing an answer (feeling stupid)
- Forgetting a key deliverable (feeling unreliable)
- Misunderstanding something (feeling dumb)
- Getting critical feedback (evidence we suck)
- Feeling patronized (inferior/unworthy)
- Feeling like a fraud (imposter syndrome)
- Seeing someone succeed (highlights our lack)
- The whole money thing (we're not worthy)

How do you feel when you read this list? Some items may be *meh*, and some may make your temperature rise. For many entrepreneurs, especially women, messing up is a sure path to shame and our current culture has created an unattainable ideal for us to chase. We hear, "If you're not making massive passive income from your business while raving fans celebrate your greatness, you aren't doing it right!"

There are people enjoying great success in their laptop lifestyle, but that doesn't mean they're *your* barometer for success. You get to decide what you want success for you to be, and then set out to reach your own level of happiness and achievement. Their journey is theirs; your journey is yours. Comparing ourselves to any other entrepreneur can touch on multiple hot buttons, pushing us deeper into Winter.

Plus, our hot buttons can keep us in Winter for too long because we live in a hyper-reactive world where our mistakes are magnified and every comment, post, photo, or review lasts forever. When we're in Winter, the negative feedback keeps providing 'evidence' of our personal and professional failures.

Let's explore what I call the *leaky window*. Imagine a storm of harsh criticism or sharp judgment is whirling and swirling ferociously outside. If we had well-insulated windows that closed up tight (how we would be if we were in Summer, feeling confident and self-assured), all that negativity and nastiness wouldn't get in. Too often, though, our windows are old (our lifelong feelings of unworthiness) and the seals around our windows are cracked (we have low self-confidence). In these times, our leaky window doesn't shut out all the stormy conditions (like judgement and nastiness) and Winter gets in.

Winter has massive power and our unresolved hot button issues are the reason we both slide into Winter *and* why we stay there. Sometimes, a hot button issue can pummel us suddenly, like one day we find a scathing testimony slamming our business and we crumble. Other times, though, our hot button was first pushed years before and it lingers just under the surface, waiting for every opportunity to say, "See? Of course I messed up. I knew it! I'm a failure."

> *"You'll never speak to anyone more than you speak to yourself. Be gentle, loving and kind."*
> ~ *Author Unknown*

How Do You React in a Storm?

When stormy weather rolls into our lives, we feel it immediately. Even if these are work-related storms, they can feel heavy, emotional, and very personal.

When you know yourself, your limits, and your needs, you can step back and see *the whole picture*.

The Whole Picture

Seeing the whole picture isn't always easy because there's never one simple cause for Winter.

It's a perfect storm of emotions and expectations. In an ideal world, we'd evaluate every situation from a bird's eye view, but business ownership *isn't* perfect. Sometimes as entrepreneurs we're barely hanging on by a thread. We're on edge and we hear one thing that sends us into reaction-mode.

In times like these, when we're struggling in some way, it's important not to get frustrated, or angry, but get curious first. Ask the *who, what, where, when, why, and how* questions. Fill in the blanks with facts, not fabrications, and see the whole picture.

Are you really having a bad day? Or has it been thirty tough minutes where your wildly negative thoughts trampled your spirit and blinded you from seeing that you do have the power, resources, and tenacity to get through it? Maybe you just need a second? Don't forget—when you control your thoughts, you control your life.

When we're on edge, stretched too thin, and the straw that cracks the camel's back lands on us, we don't always have the bandwidth to see the whole picture. We zero in on that thing that just happened, that thing that sent our blood pressure soaring. When that happens, and we're stuck on one small part of the whole issue, we're Spotlighting.

Spotlighting

Have you ever been to a theater production?

Think about the deep, dark stage. The orchestra swells. The curtains rise. A thin spotlight creates a perfect circle on the black stage. The audience is silent until you hear footsteps. Into the spotlight appears a single performer illuminated by the stream of light. You see her face, her hair, and the top part of her shimmering dress. She stands in the spotlight and sings. After a mesmerizing moment, all the stage lights burst on. Dozens of people, tons of props, and an entire set fill the stage. You didn't see any of it a moment before because of the spotlight.

Let's try this exercise. You can be in a coffee shop, at your office, on a bus, or waiting for an appointment, you can do this anywhere. We'll do something for thirty seconds so please set a timer on your phone or find a watch that measures seconds. When we start the timer, you will study your space and make a mental note of every red item in your space.

Ready? Start the thirty seconds!

When the time is over, close your eyes and tell me everything you saw that was green. Yes, green.

Most likely, you were so focused on the red items that you can't recall any or many green items. When we look for something, we don't see other things. When we spotlight, or focus on one small portion of a bigger entity, we miss things.

With that in mind, let's go back and think about one of your entrepreneurial experiences with Winter.

Did you spotlight?

Did you focus on one small thing and ignore everything else, or not see the whole picture?

In times of conflict, people develop tunnel vision. We're unable to see other possibilities besides the one in our mind. It becomes our truth, whether it's based in fact or in fiction.

Entrepreneurs frequently spotlight when they receive a negative review. It often doesn't matter if they have 100 very satisfied customers, or great working relationships with partners, or if the disgruntled person even has a legitimate complaint, one piece of negative feedback can send us to Winter.

Latisha is an esthetician specializing in lashes. She has a wall full of photos of very happy women (and a few men) proudly showing off their new lashes, with cards and testimonials praising her great work. Her calendar is booked for weeks and she has a waiting list. She spoke with her business coach who suggested Latisha consider raising her prices. Although she felt nervous, she bumped up her fee a few dollars.

One day, a client mentioned she had seen a bad review pop up about Latisha online. She found it and remembered this client, Tamara. This woman was forty-five minutes late and she didn't call or text. When she arrived, she demanded that Latisha honor her appointment even though the spa was busy all afternoon and all her other clients were all showing up on time. Latisha told her if she didn't want to come back, she would need to wait to be squeezed in. Another woman overheard the situation and graciously offered to come another day to help Latisha open up a slot. Tamara then demanded a discount on her lashes because she had to wait twenty minutes.

For days, all Latisha thought about were ways she could have done things differently, what she should have done to prevent Tamara from writing such a bad review. Latisha was spotlighting. She couldn't see any of the smiling faces on the wall, or the dozens of positive reviews. She only saw this one spiteful review. She was stuck in Winter and full of doubt, worry, feelings of inadequacy, and shame around her pricing.

Latisha responded online explaining that Tamara showed up forty-five minutes late, another client rescheduled to give Tamara her spot, and Tamara even happily posed for a photo after her appointment. Tamara responded and agreed she was happy with the lashes, but Latisha's prices were robbery and others offered better service at a better price.

She was further crushed when a client said Tamara was telling everyone in her social circle to stop coming to Latisha's salon. This now-frazzled esthetician gave her kind client a 50% discount for letting her know and she decided to call Tamara and give her two free services to make her happy again. She was spiraling and panicking, and she couldn't see in the storm.

When we fall into the deepest, darkest storms, something beyond Winter, we know we've encountered a blizzard.

Beware of the Blizzard

A blizzard is one of the harshest storms in nature, with heavy snow, brutal winds, low temperatures, and extremely limited visibility.

You experience a blizzard when your emotions drown out other thoughts and feelings and severe fear grips us. Since we're the sum of every single thought, action, interaction, feeling, and experience we've ever had, we carry every trouble, triumph, sadness, and success in our cells. These can surface and create a blizzard after months, years, or even decades.

Blizzards will be different for every person because we each bring our own occurrences, beliefs, values and secrets to our business journey. What may be a blizzard for one person could be a Winter condition for another, but there's no denying the force and severity of a blizzard in your life.

In my experience, the deepest blizzard conditions arise for most women entrepreneurs around two key blocks: money and imposter syndrome.

Money Mindset

Few topics live in the shadows of our culture that have the power to create blizzards of shame, secrecy and embarrassment. Money is one of them!

Your money mindset describes your beliefs and attitudes about money. It also shapes what you believe you can and can't do with money, as well as the amount you earn, spend, save, invest and donate.

Going even further, your money mindset influences your attitudes about other people and their money too. Many of our beliefs about money were formed in childhood while observing and internalizing messages we heard from our parents and other adults. Think about things you might have heard as a child:

- Money means trouble.
- Who do you think you are?
- Money doesn't grow on trees.
- Money doesn't buy happiness.
- People like us don't get ahead.
- Good people don't crave money.
- People won't like us if we're rich.
- Our family isn't lucky with money.
- Rich people are greedy and selfish.
- There's only so much to go around.
- Do you think we're made of money?
- I couldn't make more than your father.
- Men make the money, women spend it.

Do any of these statements sound familiar? I can hear my mom's voice saying some of these, and my dad's voice saying some other ones, as if it were yesterday. You likely had some of these money messages planted in your life too!

When we're in Winter, feeling unworthy, unable, or unqualified to be successful, the money topic can absolutely keep us in our own self-induced stormy blizzards. For Latisha, the money message that hit her hardest was *Who do you think you are?*

When she read Tamara's feedback questioning her worth, she did the only thing she could think of to get out of the blizzard: she cut her prices. She couldn't possibly be worth the amount she was charging.

Her inner critic screamed, *"You've gotten away with it long enough. Someone called you out. You've been caught. Put that price down. You might be worth the lower price but you sure as heck aren't worth the higher one! Who do you think you are to charge what you're charging? You think you're all that? You aren't."*

The initial negative feedback challenged her value. Hearing that she was robbing her clients and not worth her fee sent her into her blizzard.

Latisha isn't alone. Many entrepreneurs, especially in the beginning, claim their fiercest blizzards swirl around money. Katerina, a fashion blogger and up-and-coming designer, shared about her own tumultuous money journey.

Katerina's parents were wonderful and in love when Katerina was growing up. Her mom Talia stayed home and cooked, cleaned, and sewed pretty dresses for her, teaching her how to create new clothes out of her old clothes. Her dad Tomas worked as an electrician in town. Katerina had everything she needed. Life was great.

One day, her father was injured at work and he needed time to recover. Her mom found a job at a fashion store to help make ends meet. Katerina said her mom loved to touch the fabric and see how they fit on all the different women.

But at home, life wasn't great anymore.

Her parents fought all the time. Tomas yelled that Talia was wasting all his money on haircuts, fancy clothes, and expensive makeup. He claimed all these things were changing her into someone he didn't like.

"You aren't the wonderful wife I married! Now you're greedy, shallow, and only care about yourself."

One night he ferociously cracked the heel off one of Talia's shoes while screaming, "You will not be the kind of woman to wear these street-walking shoes!" The fighting continued until Katerina's dad moved out and left them all alone. They struggled for years.

Like her mother, Katerina loved fashion. After a few surprising twists, she found her passion as a fashion blogger and dress designer. She loved to touch all the fabrics and create dresses for real women.

All day and night, she was surrounded by fancy clothes, gorgeous heels, and priceless jewelry but she refused to wear anything but black turtlenecks, black pants, and flat shoes. She won awards and was celebrated for her beautiful designs, but she never knew the feeling of wearing one of her own garments.

As her success grew, she started sabotaging her partnerships and business relationships. She lost revenue, promotional opportunities, and professional advancement. She often gave her clothes away without even covering the cost of fabric and materials. Katrina didn't connect the dots from the intense messaging as a child to her decisions as an adult.

Since we know that our thoughts do many things, such as controlling our actions, creating our limiting beliefs, and building artificial barriers to our success, what we believe about money determines the success of our businesses and our lives.

If we believe money is hard to come by, or there isn't enough for everyone, then we won't make all the right moves. We won't call the whole list of clients. We won't try to show our value to prospective clients because we might think, "What's the point?" Then, we won't close the deal or sell the thing or achieve success or reach our potential. It will validate that we weren't worthy or capable in the first place.

That was where Katerina found herself, fully engulfed in a long-standing blizzard, questioning everything that she knew to be true. It took significant inner work to unpack so many childhood messages. With time, she realized that her father was angry and hurt, but not right. When she was able to rewrite her money messaging, she was able to step into her success as a fashion designer and beauty insider.

Katerina's mindset blocks are common, and they prevent us from taking leaps, and trying new strategies to develop. Not to mention market or sell our offerings, receive money for our time, expertise, skills, and talents, and trust that we can do it.

Do you trust you can do it? Or do you suffer from the second biggest cause of entrepreneurial blizzards?

Imposter Syndrome

Search for this term and you will see dozens of articles in high-powered business magazines such as Forbes, Entrepreneur, Time, and Inc.

According to an article published in the *International Journal of Behavioral Science*, "An estimated 70% of people experience these impostor feelings at some point in their lives."

Coined by psychologists Drs. Clance and Imes in 1978, Imposter Syndrome refers to high-achieving individuals who completely discount their successes and feel that at any moment they will be exposed as a fraud in their job or industry.

The relationship between imposter syndrome and depression or anxiety is palpable. With this condition, self-doubt isn't just present, it's crushing. The world's top performers, scientists, astronauts, writers, and of course, entrepreneurs suffer from it. It doesn't matter what level a person is at in their life, they can still tumble into Winter by believing:

- I had better be perfect, or they'll fire me ASAP.
- It's because of my connection to this person.
- I happened to be there at the right time.
- Someone has made a really big mistake.
- They'll realize I'm really not qualified.
- It's only because they like me.
- I really don't deserve this.
- I don't belong here.
- It was all luck.

No one is superwoman, although we love to try! Striking a balance between feeling like a bit of an imposter sometimes and being able to recognize your contributions and celebrate your wins is healthy and typical for business owners.

For entrepreneurs who suffer deeply from Imposter Syndrome, they become trapped in their own personal blizzard. They struggle with intense internal storms. On the one hand, they try to earn their worth by becoming massive over-achievers, constantly trying to be the most perfect/all-knowing/all-capable contributor. They refuse help or assistance from other capable people. Any mistakes shatter their shaky confidence and can cloud their judgment.

On the other hand, any praise is dismissed and any recognition is perceived as a strategy to highlight flaws and failures[i].

Imposter Syndrome highlights a serious condition for many entrepreneurs, going straight to the heart and soul of our value and our worth. Whether it's your Winter, or your Blizzard, know that it can pass and that you aren't alone.

Being nominated for a Pulitzer Prize, winning numerous Grammy awards, garnering a Tony nomination, and receiving the National Medal of Arts and the prestigious Presidential Medal of Freedom, plus over fifty honorary degrees, did nothing to squelch the feelings of imposter syndrome in author and poet Maya Angelou:

> *"I have written 11 books, but each time I think,*
> *'Uh oh, they're going to find out now. I've run a*
> *game on everybody, and they're going to find*
> *me out.'"*

---

i If you find yourself at this point, ever, please reach out for professional help from an expert. They are a lifeline.

Imposter syndrome didn't end for her as an internationally-renowned author after the first book. Nor the second, nor the eleventh.

She faced it every single time.

Harvard Business School professor and author Amy Cuddy takes our common fear of imposter syndrome and helps us understand that it indeed will pop up again and again, sometimes in the same ways, sometimes in new ways. She writes:

"Most of us will never completely shed our fears of being fraudulent. We'll just work them out as they come, one by one. Just as I can't promise that learning about presence will give you a Zen master existence in the 'eternal now,' I can't say that you will soon shed all your impostor anxieties forever. New situations may stoke old fears; future sensations of inadequacy might reawaken long-forgotten insecurities. But the more we're aware of our anxieties, the more we communicate about them, and the smarter we are about how they operate, the easier they'll be to shrug off the next time they pop up."

We may start off looking at ourselves as entrepreneurs, but our mindset in Winter is rooted in who we are as *people*. We will see our fears, yes, and if we look a little deeper, we'll find some of the core hurts we have carried for years. Facing Winter means we might relive moments of our deepest pain, shame, or humiliation, or walk through the darkest nights of our souls yet another time. We may re-experience things that changed our lives forever. It hurts to do this, and it's hard and messy. Some people push bad experiences out of sight, out of mind. That delays the inevitable—you will experience those emotions and their intensity another time because the underlying, unresolved issues still exist.

Our sense of shame isn't about the late shipment, the typos on the presentation, the mistake on the invoice, or any of the endless possibilities that we experience. It's about *who we are in our essence*. We use shame as a weapon to cut down that essence, our truest selves, saying we're 'bad' or 'broken' or 'unworthy' of love, acceptance or success. It speaks to our deepest fears that we're failing in some way, and we'll be judged harshly by those around us. So shame keeps us in Winter, and we believe there's no way out. That's just not true.

> *"Not all storms come to disrupt your life, some come to clear your path."*
>
> ~ *Author Unknown*

When You're Ready to Leave Winter

Winter can last a very short time, or it can plague us for what seems like forever. Sometimes I consult with people who've been in Winter for weeks because they had forgotten they had the power to leave. Winter has a way of keeping the negative emotions swirling.

Think of it like this: one day snow falls (conflict occurs/problem arises) but it doesn't melt because the temperatures stay below freezing (issue isn't solved). No new snow falls, but sharp winds keep swirling the fallen snow, creating endless Winter. As it sometimes happens, we can stay in Winter because one conflict keeps whirling around long after the snow fell.

In Winter, the cold, dark, reality means it's time to reflect on our behavior.

Getting out of Winter, with integrity and authenticity, requires a level of honesty you may not ever imagined. You have to dig deep. You have to uncover the wounds. You have to experience again the awful things so you can release them once and for all. There is nothing easy about realizing that you're the biggest obstacle in your way. It may be the hardest thing you've done in a long time. My life has been chock-full of hard things but doing the work to really break my own Winter patterns has been one of the most complex and emotional journeys of my life.

Some people say Winter feels too severe and uncomfortable and thus we should avoid it at all costs. I disagree. If we choose to live authentically, we'll always experience Winter because it's part of our full human experience. And, Winter has some benefits:

- Brings simmering issues to the surface
- Generates healthy conversation
- Stimulates problem solving
- Provides opportunities for diverse points of view
- Increases our understanding of issues
- Draws attention to something that needs fixing
- Shows you what you need to change to grow
- Motivates you to form new, healthier habits

We don't want to remove Winter! Instead, we strive to reduce the frequency, duration, and intensity of this crucial season.

In moments of hurt, fear, or in times when we're pushed or stressed, our worries rise to the surface. We put up our defenses and operate in survival mode—but we shouldn't stay there. When we're ready to reconnect to our brilliance, we're ready for Spring.

> *"Even if today may seem to be a time of total darkness, it will not last forever. The dawn will surely come if you advance, ever forward, without being defeated. The day will come when you can look back fondly and declare, "I am savoring this happiness because I struggled back then." It is those who know the bitterness of winter that can savor the true joy of spring."*
>
> **~ Daisaku Ikeda, Author**

CHAPTER 3

Spring

SPRING IS THE SEASON OF NEW BEGINNINGS.

*A*fter *a harsh winter,* spring brings cleansing rains to wash away the heaviness. In *The 5 Seasons of Connection to Your Business Brilliance,* Spring welcomes lightness, possibility, hope, confidence, courage, strength, boldness, and renewal.

What is Spring?

Spring is the bridge between Winter and Summer. In Spring, we feel:

- Free from the emotional weight of Winter
- Ready to soothe our spirits to be our best selves
- Grateful for Winter's gifts to move us forward
- Openness to forgive ourselves and others
- Patience/grace which leads to listening/learning
- A willingness to explore our feelings and desires
- Resurging confidence in our lives and businesses
- Bravery to show up after a period of hibernating

This season is complex because we're coming out of the most disconnected time (Winter) and moving towards the most connected time (Summer), so Spring bridges us from emotional heaviness to happiness.

It isn't enough for us to tell ourselves to be kind, or gentle, or forgiving, or patient with ourselves. We can't ignore the fact that we were just in Winter. We have to uncover what pushed us into Winter by reflecting, exploring, and giving ourselves permission to be real.

Spring is a powerful time when our fresh, hopeful, optimistic, energized *Spring-self* looks at our tired, drained, hurt, dark *Winter-self* and gets vulnerable:

> *'Thank you for swirling so ferociously to keep me safe and warm, tucked away from the world. Thank you for protecting me from risk, failure, rejection, or neglect. It's a different time now. I'm ready to push through the soil and blossom. Winter-self, join me in Spring.'*

Then you give that part of you—your protector, your inner critic, your mean girl, your itty-bitty-shitty committee— you give her something to do. So, let's put her to work.

Enter Spring Cleaning!

> *"It's time for a spring cleaning of your thoughts, it's time to stop just existing, it's time to start living."*
>
> *~ Steve Maraboli, Author*

Spring Cleaning

There's something cathartic about clearing away the build-up and debris left over from Winter and preparing for the promise of warm days and fresh air.

To find our business brilliance, we have work to do. In full transparency, some of this work will be easy for you, and some will require heavy (emotional) lifting.

Committing to the heavy lifting will help you push away your limiting beliefs, move your massive mental blocks, and break the patterns of your automatic negative thoughts (ANTs).

There are no shortcuts.

Just like you can't tackle your whole house all at once, you can't tackle this whole season all at once either. Spring cleaning happens in phases.

I break it into two parts: internal and external.

Without question, spring-cleaning your internal chaos will be a much bigger, longer, and more intense commitment than your external cleanup. Getting to our business brilliance is *absolutely* an inside job!

Think of the principles listed below as gorgeous wildflowers growing in a field. They're all beautiful, but you don't need every flower to make a stunning bouquet. Select the ones that resonate with you the most right now to keep you moving through Spring. Put the rest aside for when you are ready for more.

Internal Spring Cleaning

Our first commitment to step fully into Spring is to focus on our mind, body, and spirit first, identifying places that were battered in the Winter storms and need some TLC, but not just any standard TLC.

Can you recall your first bike ride, your first swim, your first sale, your first presentation, or your first major business purchase? All of these events probably pushed you out of your comfort zone, but you did them anyways. We're about to invest in ourselves. It may seem weird and uncomfortable, do it anyways.

Internal Spring Cleaning has ten categories. Select the strategies that either propel you forward the furthest, or the ones that hold you back the most:

1. Know Your Mindset
2. Success Defined
3. Journaling
4. Gratitude
5. Forgiveness
6. Anchors
7. Reframe Your Limiting Beliefs
8. Self-Care
9. Manifesto
10. Bliss List

1. Know Your Mindset

When I hear the word *mindset*, I think of Stanford University researcher Carol Dweck and her formative book called, *Mindset: The New Psychology of Success.*

This book changed my life and my business.

According to Dweck, there are two types of mindset: fixed and growth. When you have a fixed mindset, you believe your basic intelligence, abilities, creativity, and talents don't change throughout your life. You're born with what you have and there's nothing you can do to change it. Alternatively, when you have a growth mindset, you believe your abilities, intelligence, creativity, and talents are just a starting point. You are able to improve with time and effort.

How does this impact your business brilliance?

Your business is greatly impacted by how you see yourself and the world around you.

Is Your Mindset Fixed or Growth-based?

If you have a fixed mindset, you believe deep down you can't do anything to reach the levels of success you see other people enjoy. You'll feel you can't attain greatness above your current level because it's where you are destined to stay. You won't do whatever it takes because you will think there is no point—your level of achievement can only go so high.

However, if you have a growth mindset, you will know that you can invest in education, training, and skill development to become a better entrepreneur. You'll believe you can grow to become successful through effort and determination. You know you can rewrite the limiting beliefs that hold you back from moving forward to achieve great levels of success.

To continuously grow and expand, as well as adapt to the ever-changing world of business, entrepreneurs might struggle having a few areas of fixed mindset, but we must have a growth mindset in most of our ways. There are limitless ways you can foster and develop your growth mindset. Here are six great ideas from InformED:

1. View challenges as opportunities for self-discovery and self-improvement.
2. Regularly take time for reflection. Reframe obstacles and celebrate success.

3. Foster grit to keep going when you think you can't.
4. Add the word *yet*. (I'm not a speaker, yet.) Then, do the work to become 'it.'
5. Swap the word *failing* with *learning*. ('I'm failing at how to sell' becomes 'I am learning how to sell.'
6. Take ownership of your attitude, know you're in control of your goals. Plan them, achieve them.

As with all the strategies in Spring Cleaning mode, it isn't all or nothing. Success vs failure. Growth vs fixed. There's an ebb and flow. Each of us has aspects of both growth mindset and fixed mindset and the goal isn't to be 'all growth all the time,' but to be more growth than fixed. Interestingly, a few years after her book came out, Dweck learned some people strived to hide any evidence of a fixed mindset because they were ashamed to not be in growth all the time. She wrote an article to clarify this 'False Growth Mindset.'

"[N]obody has a growth mindset in everything all the time. Everyone is a mixture of fixed and growth mindsets. You could have a predominant growth mindset in an area but there can still be things that trigger you into a fixed mindset trait. Something really challenging and outside your comfort zone can trigger it, or, if you encounter someone who is much better than you at something you pride yourself on, you can think, "Oh, that person has ability, not me." So I think we all have to look for our fixed-mindset triggers and understand when we are falling into that mindset."

2. Success Defined

When it's time to spring clean our bathroom, we can visualize what it will look like when we're done: shiny tiles, sparkling fixtures, and a clean throne.

When it's time to Spring Clean our mindset, we have to know what we want the finished product to look like when we're done. At the end of it all, what will we have? We can't just wish for 'more of this' or 'less of that.' We need to be confident enough to state our true desires so we know what we're working towards. Otherwise, if we're wishy-washy or non-specific, how will we ever know if we got there?

Great Britain's Roger Bannister was very clear about what success meant for him. He set out to break a barrier that had eluded runners since . . . forever: running a four-minute mile.

Experts said it was impossible.

Doctors said it was dangerous.

Runners said it couldn't be done.

Then, on a windy day in May 1954, Bannister achieved his goal and set a first-time world record by reaching the one mile mark at 3:59.4. Some people use the story of Bannister's achievement to demonstrate the power of the human spirit, but the truth is that he *wanted* to run that time. He *trained* to run that time. As a medical student, he studied anatomy, physiology and nutrition to understand *how* he could run that time.

Not seven weeks later, Australian runner John Landy broke Bannister's time running at 3:58.0. The two faced off in Vancouver later that year in what was called, "The Race of The Century." Bannister trailed Landy until the last 90 yards when he zipped ahead to finish at 3:58.8 to Landy's 3:59.6, the first time two runners ran under four minutes in the same race.

Even though everyone said it couldn't be done, Bannister got very clear on what success meant to him and every decision supported his goal. Landy defined success the same way and he also reached his goal.

When you ask beginning entrepreneurs what benchmark would show success in their business, the quick and easy answer is, "Money!" But, pretty quickly entrepreneurs set other benchmarks for success.

Ask yourself, *what is it all about for you?*

To be honest, some of us could make more money with less stress if we had a corporate job. But, we're entrepreneurs, we want to make our own magic. We want to create and control our time, energy, and resources. We don't want FINE. We want exceptional. We want impactful, meaningful work. We want to reach our amazing life goals.

What is Success for Me?
I'll be successful when I have _____
____ This amount of money (how much?)
____ Considerable wealth for my family
____ Personal growth and development
____ Fame
____ Power
____ Wisdom
____ Influence
____ Fancy things
____ More free time

_____ A focus on doing good
_____ Ability to live my purpose
_____ A career where I am my own boss

Was this harder than it seemed?

Sure, you go into business for yourself for many reasons, money being a big one. But, if you had tons of money and felt trapped, would you feel successful? If you made buckets of money but your client was skirting the edge of what is legal, ethical, or moral, would you feel successful? If you made enough money being your own boss to have time to play with your kids and take great vacations, would that be success?

To find your true definition of success, we need to think into the future.

Who is Future Me?

Think about your life five years from now. Your ideal life. The life you dream about. The life that would be the very best it could be for you. Here we go!

It's five years in the future. You wake up slowly, with the rising sun shining into your bedroom. Who is with you? What are you wearing? What color is your room, and what décor have you chosen? What does your bed look like? What do you see when you look around?

You walk through your house toward the kitchen. What is hanging on your walls? What shoes sit by your front door? What rooms do you pass?

You prepare your favorite beverage. What's in your cup? What will you eat for breakfast? Who are you with?

It is glorious outside and you're eager to start your day. How do you spend your morning? What do you do first? What's most exciting today? Who do you do it with? You are so grateful that your morning is what you always dreamed it to be. What is the best part of your morning?

It's lunchtime now. You're hungry. Where are you going to eat? What will you have? Who will you eat with? Is your lunch leisurely or on-the-go?

After lunch, you smile when you see that it's time for your magic hour, time you have blocked in your calendar for nurturing your passion and creative flow. What are you doing during this hour? What are you creating? How are you creating it? When it's done, what will it look like? What will it feel like?

You return to put in a few more hours of work. What does your workspace look like? What are you working on? How does your afternoon unfold? Are you in meetings, collaborating with others? Are you working on something on your own? Are you with clients? Investors?

Before the end of your day, you receive big news about your business you weren't expecting, making your heart fill with joy, gratitude and fulfillment.

Oh, it was a great day! You did exactly what you love, tapping into your unique passions and genius and you positively impacted people you serve in your business. Today was amazing. What wonderful things did your business allow you to do for others? Who did you serve? What solutions did you provide that made a difference?

You arrive home and as you come into your driveway, you smile. Home. Your place of peace, calm, serenity, and joy. Who is there waiting for you? What does your evening look like tonight, on your ideal night? Is a quiet dinner for a few people, or are you in a large group? Who will share your meal with you? How do you wrap up your glorious day? What rituals do you have that you love?

The sun has long set, the evening is over and you're going to bed. You look around your house and you feel so much joy and love. Who shares your home with you? Are they with you now? What amazing things has your business been able to provide for your family and life?

As you climb into your dream bed, at the end of your ideal day, you look out your window and think, *Thank you. Today was a great day.* You say a silent prayer. What emotions and feelings do you express? What was in your prayer? What were your final thoughts as you drifted off to sleep? What are your hopes for tomorrow? What do you want to experience this week that makes your heart fill with joy and anticipation?

This was your ideal day, a compilation of your wishes for your future. Your definition of success is in this story. I love to visualize my ideal day once or twice a year to see if new things pop up for me.

What are some of the things that popped into your mind as you imagined your ideal day in five years?

Were you surprised where you lived?

Did you notice the car you drove?

Were you amazed at how you spent your time?

What was the great news you received?

What were your final gratitudes before bed?

To help you complete this visualization, complete the following statements. (You can write in the book!)

Future me (FM) is _____

FM loves _____

FM values _____

FM wants more _____

FM wants less _____

FM shines brightest when _____

FM's business focuses on _____

FM's business successes are _____

FM believes success is _____

FM has found her purpose in _____

_____

_____

How fun was that?

Identifying What Stands in Your Way

Another exercise I have used to define success for me is called "If I had... I would" brainstorming.

Sometimes, the path to our goals is blocked. In this next exercise, remove the real (or not-so-real) blocks so you can see what success means to you.

Here are a few examples:

If I had $2000 per month, **I would** hire help.

(success = a level of freedom)

If I had free time, **I would** write a book.

(success = creating a legacy to educate)

If I had huge profits, **I would** donate more.

(success = bigger philanthropy)

What would you do if nothing stood in your way?

If I had _____ I would _____

If I had _____ I would _____

If I had _____ I would _____

How you define your success is up to you.

If you believe that you'll reach success when you have power and influence, then all the material items in the world won't make you feel successful. If success means donating money to a worthy cause, winning awards won't bring you fulfilment.

As the day slides into night, and the moon waxes and wanes through all its phases, know that your journey will ebb and flow along your entrepreneurial path too. Defining what success means to you will set the destination on your internal GPS, so you don't spin in place. Until you know where you're going, you may just be busy going nowhere. The process of reaching success is often a long-term one.

Being an entrepreneur isn't an overnight commitment, so I know you're in this for the long ride.

3. Journaling

Journaling is one of the most powerful ways to Spring Clean your mind and spirit, as well as prepare you to reconnect to your own brilliance. This practice has the potential to rise above all others on your Spring journey because it's where you get real, honest, and vulnerable with yourself. You can shed your self-protection masks and armor and be truly, madly, deeply you. Plus, capturing your ideas, thoughts, feelings, and experiences in one place and processing them by seeing them on paper has been the habit of some of our world's best philosophers, writers, and entrepreneurs for centuries. Anne Frank, Benjamin Franklin, Leonardo da Vinci, Sir Richard Branson and Oprah Winfrey all kept/keep journals.

There are no rules for journaling. You can make it as simple or as fancy as you'd like, but the key is to write as raw, as unedited, and as honestly as you can. Be consistent. Give yourself permission to get intimate in a relationship with your true self.

On the pages of your journal, you're the author and the audience so you can remove the mask of perfection and be authentically, unapologetically you.

Other ways journaling helps:

1. Journaling helps you process differently. When something provokes your ANTs, you may feel hurt, anger, or fear, but this helps you see other angles.
2. Journaling can identify patterns over time and show you where you go when you're provoked or feeling out of control. When you read over your past entries and see the same themes, you can consciously untangle them and make changes.

3. Journaling gives you permission to dream. It clarifies your hopes and wishes, what you want to experience, and how you want to live and work.
4. Journaling tracks how far you've come. Over time, you'll see where you were, where you are now, and all that you've overcome so far.
5. Journaling strengthens your business brilliance. When you write about your passion/purpose (all Summer features), you capture the magical moments and feelings. Bookmark to help chase any impending Winter days away.

Think of journaling like this: it's like that time in summer when you collected extra berries to make jam. Jam isn't exactly the same as the fresh fruit but tasting it can whisk you back to those great days when you picked them fresh in the sun. Your journal can take you back to the best moments of yourself.

Journaling is extra effort in a busy and demanding day, I know. We're entrepreneurs, and we're moms, wives, sisters, miracle-makers, and life-changers. We're busy people! Yet, a commitment to journaling is a promise for personal growth unlike any other methods.

4. Gratitude

We talk a lot about gratitude for good reason!

Science shows people who practice gratitude regularly enjoy more restful sleep, increased energy, enhanced decision making, better productivity, higher goal achievement, and improvements to social behaviors which help develop relationships in personal and business environments.

However, gratitude is much more powerful than we even thought, especially in helping us transform our mindset from stormy to successful. Gratitude releases us from the chains of toxic and damaging emotions by helping us reframe something dark and stormy into something lighter and calmer.

A Spring silver lining, if you will.

There's a difference between *feeling* grateful and *being* grateful. We won't always *feel* grateful, like when we lose a major client, or when a piece of equipment breaks beyond repair, but we can *be* grateful that we now have space in our schedule to book a new client, or *be* grateful that the damage was only to that one piece of equipment.

Having an attitude of gratitude mindset twists our kaleidoscope just enough so everything we see looks different. Gratitude is a state of Summer.

> *"It is not happy people who are grateful; it is grateful people who are happy."*
> ~ **Author Unknown**

5. Forgiveness

Holding onto old hurts and not forgiving yourself or others can impact your business brilliance by keeping you feeling disempowered in deep ways.

Psychologists define forgiveness as *a conscious, deliberate decision to release feelings of resentment toward a person or group who has harmed you, regardless of whether they deserve your forgiveness.*

This isn't about *if* the offender deserves it.

True forgiveness isn't about the other person, or about your role. It's about unshackling yourself from the burden in your heart, mind, and soul.

Some people live their whole lives holding onto past hurt, pain, and trauma. As new hurts arise, they pile it on top, deepening their own pain and suffering. We even suffer physical manifestations of our emotional pain, such as higher blood pressure, higher stress hormones, decreased sleep, increased depression, and more aches and pains.

To be fully in Spring, you need to forgive. Time will not heal your wounds because the mere passage of time isn't enough. Forgiveness is active, not passive. Healing the wounds takes work. It takes reflection.

Cassandra smiles at me as she sits in her office, looking out at a park across the street. On her desk, I see a picture of an old table with fabric piled up, in what looks like a warehouse.

Being curious, I asked if she would be open to telling me the story behind that photo.

"This picture was taken decades ago. I grew up poor, but as a teen, I worked at a local sewing shop and I learned how to make clothes. When I turned 19, I felt ready to quit my job and open my own dress shop.

"I found the only space I could afford: a tiny room in a run-down warehouse. I spent every penny to buy reams of gorgeous fabric. My friend took this picture as the *before,* but we never got to the *after.*

A few days later, a fire burned the warehouse down. I lost everything. Because it was a sort-of abandoned warehouse, no one investigated but the fireman told me an iron likely sparked the fire. I literally set fire to my own dreams. I burned every thread of fabric I had worked years to buy, and the entire building. The guilt and shame were profound.

"I shamefully went back to work in the sewing shop. Eventually, I made a dress for my mom, then another, but my mistake haunted me every day. I checked my irons four or five times a day. I put reminders on my mirrors and by my bed so I would never forget again. My sister recommended therapy to get over my terrible panic and raging guilt.

"No lie, it was really hard. I thought if I forgave myself, I was giving myself a free pass, denying my responsibility for my mistake. But I learned self-forgiveness is about taking responsibility in a healthy way. I couldn't rebuild the warehouse, but I now donate some of my sales to a design school scholarship so new designers are trained in the basics, like safety.

"I found a way to forgive myself. This picture isn't here to shame me; it's here to remind me that even the most disastrous mistakes are just that—mistakes. We can forgive mistakes."

~ Cassandra, fashion designer

"The weak can never forgive. Forgiveness is the attribute of the strong."

*~ **Mahatma Gandhi, Civil Rights Leader***

6. Anchors

We talk about the beauty and possibility of Spring, but this transitional season also experiences some lingering cold snaps and endless days of rain.

When we haven't quite arrived at Summer's doorstep, we need something that reminds us of the glorious days to come when we believe in our worth, our value, and our ability to create positivity through our business offerings.

Those things are anchors.

Anchors keep boats from drifting off during the night or during rough weather. In our lives, anchors are those things that make us feel grounded and connected to the best version of ourselves.

It could be a person, place, or an item that feeds your soul. Anchors bring a sense of peace, purpose, and meaning when the winds swirl around you.

Think about the anchors in your life; maybe the picnic table at the park where you created your first business plan, or a photo of a loved one who believed in your dreams. Maybe it's a service award from your business community, or maybe it's your mentor who guides you through all the seasons of your business.

> *"Life's roughest storms proves the strengths of our anchor."*
>
> *~ Author Unknown*

Jacinta owns a pastry company and owes a part of her success to a sweet relationship she nurtured over two decades with Cindy, the owner of a coffee shop. They formed a partnership where Jacinta would use Cindy's commercial kitchen three times per week for her own business, and as payment she would create 150 items for Cindy to sell.

For years, the women grew their families, businesses, and a beautiful friendship based on collaboration, love and support. Then, Cindy fell sick. Her adult son took over the shop and things changed.

He told Jacinta, "I want to rent the kitchen to other folks too, so we're cutting you from three days to two, and you need to put your stuff away from now on. Plus, we'll need more items, 150 isn't enough for the value of a commercial kitchen anymore. Let's add some gluten-free options, can you do some eclairs?"

All of a sudden, Jacinta was thrown into a massive storm. She had to cut back on her clients because she only had kitchen access twice a week. She cleaned more diligently after her shifts to leave no trace, left extra of what she made, and spent valuable time trying to create gluten-free eclairs, but she just couldn't get them right so her inner critic started to scream: *I can't run a pastry business if I can't make pastry,* and *I'm not a great businesswoman if I can't be agile to change.*

In business and in life, Cindy and Jacinta were always there for each other, through their stormiest Winters and their most sparkling Summers. Jacinta was aching for her friend, so she went to visit Cindy.

Immediately, both women felt better just being together. Jacinta was saddened to hear that Cindy was left alone day and night and didn't really have a strong will to fight. Cindy was heartbroken to hear of the changes at her shop that were pushing Jacinta to consider closing her business. Even amidst their own storms, when they were together, they felt peace. They were each other's anchors.

Who are the people, what are the things, and where are the places that serve as your anchor?

My anchors are

_____

_____

How do your anchors help you?

_____

_____

If you don't have anchors yet, what will you choose?

_____

_____

7. Reframe Your Limiting Beliefs

When I first heard about 'reframing,' I didn't think it applied to me. I was a new entrepreneur, bubbly and excited about all the new things I was experiencing. Sometimes, I even felt unstoppable.

One warm April day, I met with a woman who had been very successful in business for many years. I happily shared about organizing my first conference, and all the cool things I was planning and creating.

After listening for some time, she said I was destined to always struggle because I was crippled by my own limiting beliefs. "That can't be! I don't want to struggle!" I insisted. She replied, "You don't trust yourself enough to succeed. Like just now, you asked me how I'd decide on things you've already decided."

I started to challenge her, but she was right; I wanted her stamp of approval on everything. Even though her business model, demographics and skillset were totally different than mine, I was willing to do things the way she said she would do them in my situation because I was sure she knew better than me. Thankfully, she nudged me with questions instead of answers and I learned a lot that day.

One lasting lesson is when we have these limiting, fear-based thoughts, we need to reframe them.

> *"It has taken me quite a few years to realize most of the thoughts in my head are not necessary."*
> ~ **Bert McCoy, Author**

Reframing is a technique to change a negative thought, or limiting belief, into a positive one. It sounds simple, but it can be really challenging.

For me, part of the issue was I didn't recognize that my thoughts were negative or limiting in any way. They were just the way I saw things.

For example, a few of my limiting beliefs were:

- Moms are too busy to come to my events.
- They won't pay to hear an unknown person
- Women don't want to hang out with strangers.
- I don't know how I would ever sell tickets
- Who would give up family time for me?
- I'm not a speaker, who am I to be on stage?

We've all thought things like this about our businesses. Things that seemed right and rational. But, after hearing my friend point out the ways I could benefit from reframing, I realized I had work to do.

This is how I reframed some of my limiting beliefs:

- Moms often live/work/exist in isolation and they need time away from their lives to have a mental break, meet new people, and learn new ideas.
- We crave real stories of grit and inspiration
- I'm providing a safe, supportive, encouraging, fun space where women can learn, share, and connect.
- I've been sharing my story in small groups for years. I'm ready to speak on a stage.

We're so 'in it' that it often takes an outsider to point out our fear-based excuses. Spring Cleaning is the time when we get rid of those excuses to uncover our confidence and our business brilliance. Although it helps to have an outsider to point out our limiting beliefs, sometimes we just need to go back to the very beginning and analyze the journey with fresh eyes.

In the book *Blue Ocean Shift*, the authors explore how reframing helped a big company challenge everything about their business to rise above their competition and be the leader in their field.

French multi-national firm Group SEB makes small appliances and they were losing tons of money on one product in particular- the French Fry maker. They were experiencing increased competition, very low profit margins, and rising usage costs for the customer (their current fryer used a whopping 2.5 liters (0.6 gallons) of fresh oil per use). Plus, the market was decreasing 10% per year because people were eating healthier. Things were looking grim.

They decided to go to the very beginning of their product's story and challenge its most fundamental beliefs: French fries require frying, and frying uses lots of oil. These limiting beliefs kept them in tight competition for years. Challenging these, though, opened a whole world of possibility. Their ability to reframe the problem changed everything.

In 2006, they launched ActiFry, an appliance requiring no frying and needing only one tablespoon of oil per use. On top of that, the fries were delicious. It gained the attention of Oprah Winfrey who tweeted her love of this product, causing a surge of purchases. This product only exists because Group SEB reframed their limiting beliefs and started with fresh eyes.

What are some basic beliefs about your industry, your clients, your packages, your products, your marketing, or your customer relations that you could challenge and see in a new way, in a new frame?

In the space provided, write a limiting belief you hold about your business, then scan the ideas below and select the best technique to reframe it.

What are some strategies to reframe?

If/then

Limiting belief: No one wants or needs my product.

Reframe: I'll email my list about my product launch and let my clients decide if this is a solution they want or need. Some people love to buy the newest products, some might buy as a gift. I'll let them decide.

Find your superpower
Limiting belief: I'm too young/old to start a business.

Reframe: I will find some *Top 30 Under 30/Top 50 Over 50*-type of articles, or watch videos of entrepreneurs who used their age to their advantage to achieve great success.

Life is an Education too
Limiting belief: I don't have a college degree.

Reframe: I can be like other innovators and solution-creators who use their intuition, instincts, life and work experiences to impact lives without a degree.

Take a bird's eye view
Limiting belief: I can't publish until it's perfect.

Reframe: If there's a woman sitting on her bathroom floor, crying and dying inside because she's in her personal Winter, could my book help her through her dark and stormy times right now? If the answer is *yes*, then *done well* is better than *perfect* and I will not wait any longer. Someone needs my book today.

Confront it Head On
Limiting belief: I can't get it all done, I'm just too slow.

Reframe: Am I sure about this? Do I really believe this? Or did the project balloon out of control and the time I set aside is no longer adequate? I'm not slow after all.

Imagine a dear friend called you with the exact limiting beliefs in your mind. Would you agree with her and say, 'Yes, Chloe, don't even bother trying, you're too old/too imperfect/too slow?' Most likely you would help her reframe her anxieties to find the silver lining or encourage her to take the risk. Just as you would encourage Chloe to harness her business brilliance, reframing allows you to harness yours. With the energy you have, what can you do? With the resources you have, what can you do?

> *"No beating yourself up. That's not allowed. Be patient with yourself. It took you years to form the bad habits of thought that you no longer want. It will take a little time to form new and better ones. But I promise you this: Even a slight move in this direction will bring you some peace. The more effort you apply to it, the faster you'll find your bliss."*
>
> *~ Holly Mosier, Author*

8. Self-Care = Self-Love

Self-care has become a media buzzword—but it isn't just about massages and manicures. True self-care is being the healthiest version of ourselves, boosting our sense of well-being.

We may have descended into Winter for many reasons, but one common reason is that we depleted our spiritual, emotional, or physical reserves below the healthy limit. When we live to give it all away as an entrepreneur, parent, or person in our community without nourishing ourselves, we risk going to Winter.

Self-care can take many forms, but ultimately when we invest in self-care, we're choosing to honor and cherish our whole selves—spiritually, emotionally, physically, relationally, intellectually, and occupationally. Strong self-care practices nourish us, and as a result, they allow us to be our best selves for ourselves and for the people who benefit from our personal and professional offerings.

"Self-care is never a selfish act - it is simply good stewardship of the only gift I have, the gift I was put on earth to offer others. Anytime we can listen to true self and give the care it requires, we do it not only for ourselves, but for the many others whose lives we touch."

~ Parker Palmer, Author

If self-care is so important, why do we neglect it? Often, it's deemed a luxury. When faced with choices on how to allocate time, energy, or money, we often opt to cut out self-care. When this is the case, we have placed other people's well-being above our own. It isn't because we don't want to nourish ourselves. It's more likely we lack a strong sense of self-worth.

Self-Worth

Self-worth comes from awareness, understanding, love, and acceptance of oneself. It's a direct measure of how much you value yourself, your strengths, talents. struggles, and limitations.

If you have high self-worth, you have an unshakable faith in yourself and you feel worthy and deserving of happiness, health, wealth, success and love.

In contrast, if you have low self-worth, if you don't think you're worthy of attention, investment, or success. Those with low self-worth also undervalue their time, devalue their offerings, and live in financial hardship because deep down they don't believe they deserve abundance.

> *"Self-worth comes from one thing – thinking that you are worthy."*
>
> ~ **Wayne Dyer, Author**

Think of everything you have in your life: your home, car, your clothes, shoes, jewelry, all your 'stuff,' your professional relationships, your business, assets, savings, and investments. Your life is full of things!

Now, what if all of it was suddenly taken away? What if all you had left was . . . you?

What would you have that would be of value?

If you have a high level of self-worth, this exercise won't change how you view your value at all because you don't derive your worth from external sources. Alternatively, if you think you'd have nothing left of value, your level of self-worth is on the low side and you may use 'things' to show the world you're worthy.

We're worthy NOT because of who we know, what we do, what we make, where we live, or what we own.

We were born worthy and we take care of ourselves because we're worthy.

Are Well-Being and Self-Care the Same?

Well-being is an all-encompassing term assessing health, happiness, and enough-ness in your life. Self-care practices, on the other hand, are the things you do to nurture your well-being. If your self-care practices are lacking, your sense of well-being will be low. When we neglect self-care, we feel:

- Exhausted
- Stressed Out
- Burnt out
- Sluggish
- Unfocussed

- Agitated
- Empty
- Craving sweet/alcohol
- Disorganized
- Impatient

We often don't realize we've treated self-care like *a luxury we can do without* until we make choices that contribute to our decline.

Huge deadline? Skip breakfast to get it done.

Late meeting? A protein shake becomes dinner.

Binging the latest show? Sleep is overrated.

Stressed out? Eat mindlessly until wine o'clock.

Wendy knows this cycle all too well. She shared her story about the price she paid for ignoring self-care.

"I run the admin side of our tree-trimming business and my husband Joe does the labor. Coming home one night, his truck was hit and he had terrible back pain and headaches. But we had clients so I went to trim.

After my first day, I felt an aching in my lower back. Maybe a pulled muscle? Next day, more pain and I felt hot so I took something. Then I cooked, cleaned, did kid stuff and business stuff so Joe could rest.

Next three days, more of the same. Day six, I was at my client's house and then I doubled over on the dirt. My client called 911. The conversation was like: *"How long have you felt pain? Six days. Any fever? Yes."*

While I was busy taking care of everyone and everything else, I didn't even notice I had a serious bladder infection that could've been solved faster and cheaper if I paid attention to my body."

~ Wendy, arbor business owner

There'll never be a time when the flight attendant tells you to put everyone else's oxygen mask on first.

Giving your business and your clients your time and energy requires you to come to the interaction nourished and ready to share your brilliance. You can't give if you are exhausted or feeling disempowered.

We know intellectually we should get more sleep, eat more veggies, spend more time outside, watch less news, and hang out with kind people to live a healthy life. However, in practice, we dismiss all this so we can work longer and harder, hurting our well-being.

We don't need to prove we're worthy or deserving entrepreneurs by powering through at all costs. We need to invest in our well-being, prioritizing excellent self-care practices so we can fully arrive in Spring. Let's see how well you are taking care of yourself.

> *"When the well's dry, we know the worth of water."*
> *~ Benjamin Franklin,*
> *Founding Father of the U.S.A.*

Self-Care Quiz

Y N   Do you have a morning practice to center you?

Y N   Do you eat healthy, nutritious food?

Y N   Do you let yourself feel uncomfortable without numbing out your feelings?

Y N   Do you exercise at least three times a week?

Y N   Do you sleep 6-8 hours a night?

Y N   Does your work stimulate your mind?

Y N   Do you spend quality, time with your partner?

Y N   Are you managing your money well?

Y N   Do you spend time on hobbies or activities?

Y N   Do you say no when you need to step back?

Y N   Do you have friends who truly understand you?

Y N   Do you use your talents in a fulfilling way?

Y N   Do you meditate, pray, or calm your thoughts?

Y N   Do you ask friends for help when you need it?

Y N   Do you have an evening routine to release your stress and prepare you for restful sleep?

Scoring   _____ Yes answers   _____ No answers

11-15 YES answers: Congrats! You've prioritized self-care and know it's critical to your wellness.

6-10 YES answers: You have some good self-care practices. When you can, add another practice.

1-5 YES answers: Oh, my friend, put you first! You are denying yourself nourishment, and investment to stay healthy and strong. You're at risk of Winter.

Is All Self-care Equal?

The short answer is no. Some practices are more vital or have greater impact at a given time. How do you know what needs care? We have a tool to help.

The Well-being Wheel

There are six unique sections that contribute to our overall sense of well-being. If any of these categories are lacking, we can't be in our brilliance.

Spiritual[ii] –meaning, purpose, prayer, meditation
Emotional – feeling the feelings, good and bad
Relational – strong bonds with other people
Physical – food, sleep, activity, stress,
Intellectual –learning, training, managing life
Occupational[iii] – using talents/skills in work

---

ii *Spirituality* is often interchanged with religion, but you can be deeply spiritual without a religious component.

iii *Occupational* self-care refers to our marketable skills we use to land a job, career, or launch/run our business.

At a glance, you might think you are doing pretty good, but if you're coming into Spring after a harsh Winter, there will be some self-care practices that could use some TLC. But which ones?

The following chart helps us identify them. It's looks simple but don't underestimate its value —it's profoundly helpful. And, there's no shame in the well-being game, so be very honest with yourself.

The first time Kay did this exercise, she filled all the boxes to the top and proudly showed how she was making self-care a top priority. I asked if she would be willing to share some self-care tips. She stared for a second and then tears sprang into her eyes.

"When I held up my chart filled to the top, no one saw I was hiding behind a mask. When Leanne asked if I could share some meaningful ways I practice self-care, it shook me to my core.

"My true self, under my mask, is spiritually tired, angry, bored, lonely, and fed-up. I looked around and I just couldn't lie anymore. I cried, releasing the pain and shame of neglecting my body, mind, and spirit in my effort to be the *perfect mom/ wife/woman.*

I did the chart again. It looked nothing like the first one but was a true and accurate reflection of my self-care. It gave me a new place to start building something real."

~ *Kay, part-time entrepreneur, mom of four*

For each category, shade how nurtured you feel:

- o is lowest (I neglect myself completely)
- 3 is low-ish (I try to do a few things a month).
- 5 is medium (I practice something every week)
- 7 is high-ish (I do a few things 3x/week)
- 10 is highest (Have a daily practice that works)

Did you uncover any revelations?

After this exercise, many entrepreneurs are shocked their score was lower than they expected, but, in reality, we don't often choose wellbeing over work or wealth. If you'd like to invest some time and energy into any of these categories, here are some ideas to get you started.

> *"The part can never be well unless the whole is well."*
>
> **~ Plato, Philosopher**

Ideas to Nourish the Six Sections of Well-being

Spiritual

- Walk in fresh air. Listen to the sounds around you.
- Light a fire and be mesmerized by the flames.
- Lay on a blanket at night and watch the night sky.
- Meditate on your own or with a guided program.
- Pray or speak what's in your heart.
- Practice random acts-of-kindness.
- Read inspirational/religious texts for hope.
- Practice mindfulness by focusing on simple items.
- Find the miracles in your day, big and small.
- Be thankful in the moment.

Emotional

- Journal without censoring or restricting ideas.
- Explore new ways to respond to hot button issues
- Set/maintain boundaries on your time and energy.
- Practice gratitude each day by naming five gifts.
- Stop harmful self-talk. Quiet your inner critic.
- Say yes to your needs. You matter very much!
- Feel big emotions. Remember—you're in control.
- Allow time to create art, sing, dance.
- Schedule white space in your day and simply *be*.
- Limit time on social media. Avoid *highlight reels.*

Relational

- Have date night. Talk about all things but kids.
- Spend quality time with people you love.
- Be around people who positively impact you.
- Volunteer in your community.
- Nurture your close, trusted friendships.
- Thank someone who made a difference.
- Find a social hobby (for the introverts)
- Call a good friend and check in with them.
- Send postcards to family when you travel.
- Organize family activities that are simple and fun.

Physical

- Stay current on your medical/dental checkups.
- Drink more water.
- Plan and prepare healthy meals and snacks.
- Commit to exercising or being active every day.
- Protect your sleeping time ferociously.
- Substitute sugar foods with natural treats.
- Take lessons in a new physical activity.
- Put scented oils/salts in bath as a stress reducer.
- Explore movement with dance/flow exercise
- When you need to cry, laugh, scream, vent—do it.

Intellectual

- Explore an art gallery. Learn about the artists.
- Visit a museum. Research the exhibits.
- Turn off news, disconnect devices, and read.
- Work on a crossword puzzle or Sudoku.

- Take a class.
- Watch a tutorial online for a DIY project.
- Learn a new musical instrument.
- Limit tabloid-type-TV. Choose documentaries.
- Use lists/apps to stay organized and productive.
- Be around smart, thoughtful dreamers.

Occupational

- Balance your work and life demands.
- Create a healthy space with vital items in reach.
- Find a mentor or be a mentor.
- Problem-solve to increase your sense of control.
- Up-level your skills for more income.
- Network with people in your field or industry.
- Be more visible to showcase your expertise.
- Assess yourself to identify skills and strengths.
- Know your industry. Stay current in your market.
- Especially for at-home-moms: know your worth.

My Self-Care Plan

Hopefully, you found some great ideas for your own self-care practices. Fill out the chart below with commitments that will nurture you the best.

Don't feel pressure to put huge, complicated items on your list. Instead, think of ways you could support your overall health and happiness by making small changes: reading an inspirational passage first thing in the morning, drinking a glass of water before your coffee, taking the stairs, turning off your phone after dinner, scheduling a date night once a month, or meeting a friend for a walk.[iv]

Use this chart to commit to and track new practices. Note the word *practice*. It isn't perfect. Celebrate every step, no matter how small, as you begin your self-care journey.

Self-Care	I will add...	And after that, I'll add...
Spiritual		
Emotional		
Physical		
Relational		
Intellectual		
Occupational		

Being fully in Spring when you've invested in your well-being allows you to release Winter's heaviness.

9. Manifesto

In my networking group, we shared affirmations we love and then used them to create a Manifesto.

---

iv   For those of us who struggle with self-worth: seek the support you need. When we hide, hibernate, or isolate ourselves too long, we forget how powerful it is to connect with others. Your friends can help you through Fall and Winter much better than you can get through on your own. Trust. Connect. Accept friend love. And if you need professional help, reach out. Therapy is a lifeline.

At first when we heard the word *manifesto*, many of us joked about old European political systems or deranged serial killers. The word derives from the Latin *manifestus*, which means *plainly clear or apparent*. A manifesto is really a declaration of what is clear and important in our lives, and it spells out a way to get there.

In other words, a manifesto functions as a bold, slightly badass, inspirational call-to-action. It's a collection of power words that pair positive thinking with action. And, it helps us capture our business brilliance when we're feeling strong and confident.

We couldn't write this in Winter. It would be gloomy and uninspired. However, now that we're in Spring, cleaning out our old limiting beliefs and mental blocks, we're ready to welcome in a gust of fresh, dynamic, empowering air to lift us up so we can soar!

When moving to the end of Spring, tapping on the door to Summer, we're really close to the happy, connected, empowered, confident feelings we seek.

The feelings we want more of.

Think of your manifesto as a glorious "This Is Who I Am As My Best Self" letter from your 'Spring self' written to your 'Winter self.' It serves as a reminder of *who we are* so we can more easily get through our challenges when the storms return.

In this Spring cleaning exercise, we'll write our own Manifesto. This exercise has a lot of power. Not only in doing, but in absorbing the words into your conscious and subconscious mind. By reading it every day and allowing it to plant its message inside our psyche, we allow it to blossom and grow.

"I only read nautical novels and my own personal manifestos."

**~ Ron Swanson,
from TV's Parks and Recreation**

Think of it this way. You want to plant flowers in your yard, but first you need to move a huge, heavy rock. One day you decide it's the day to do it. You go outside and look at it for a moment, then push it. It barely wiggles in the soil. You turn around, walk away, and hope to try again next week.

Now imagine that rock is your negative mindset.

The rock represents the words you use to shut yourself down, to keep yourself hiding, or small, or afraid to take action. That rock represents all the ways you derail your success, sabotage your progress, or mock the dreams in your mind.

One push once a week isn't going to get that rock moved any more than one time reframing a negative thought into a positive one, or one act of self-care will set new patterns for your mindset.

You're going to need to commit to working on the rock all the time. You're going to strain, and sweat, and exert a ton of force. But when you get it moving it will move easier—every push will be easier than the previous. Frequency and consistency are key, so make your Manifesto a part of your day every day. Hang it in your bathroom to read when you brush your teeth. Hang it on your fridge so you see it every time you eat. Let it soak in.

Think about it when you're at a Crossroads, deciding between growth and fear, expansion or contraction, shining or hiding. Like most things in your business and your life, (developing healthy eating habits, training for a marathon, learning piano) it's not a one-and-done.

Affirmations without action are just wishes. Remember, your Manifesto is a positive love letter FROM your confident, capable, very courageous self TO your worried, doubting, anxious, fearful self. It's advice from someone who loves you most—you!

Some tips about Manifestos:

- They are short, written in the present tense.
- They provoke some kind of transformation.
- They are motivating and inspirational.
- They offer guidance at your Crossroads.
- They help you create a new way of being.

Here are some ideas to get your creativity flowing.

- I'm enough.
- I control me.
- I live fearlessly.
- I'm unstoppable.
- I'm ready to lead.
- I trust myself first.
- My best is my best.
- I set goals for myself.
- I believe in my worth.
- I am better every day.
- My energy, my choices.

- I control my happiness.
- I focus on what matters.
- I have everything I need.
- I create the business I want.
- Money means freedom to me.
- My mistakes are my teachers.
- I choose how I spend my time.
- I am courageous and confident.
- I am tenacious and determined.
- I am positive and attract positive.
- I am stronger than any Winter storm.
- I love and respect me, first and always.
- I live authentically and unapologetically.
- I control my feelings by shifting my thoughts.
- I show up every day for my wild, beautiful life.
- I nurture my strengths and passion like a boss.
- I make my dreams come true.
- I am open and ready to grow.
- I am worthy of great success.
- I make amazing things happen.
- My light shines bright for others.

How Can You Use Your Manifesto?

Imagine you're attending a networking event with entrepreneurs who have passion and ambition just like you. They are fun, dynamic and totally real about their ups and downs. These are your people!

The leader asks if anyone knows how to solve XYZ for another member. You've solved this problem for yourself before, but you find yourself at a Crossroads.

Down one path is fear. Your coping mechanism of *hiding* kicks in and you busy yourself shuffling papers, looking down into your bag, hoping no one says your name out loud. What if your solution doesn't work? What if people dismiss your idea as too simplistic?

Down the other path is your truest and best self, holding your Manifesto. Your finger points to your promise, "My Light Shines Bright For Others." Even though you feel trepidation, your hand rises because you've solved this problem before, your experience can light the way for someone who's lost and confused.

That is who you are—a shining light, a helpful hand, a lighthouse in someone else's storm.

You honor your manifesto.

You help the member out.

She is so grateful because this kept her stuck in her Winter storm for too long. You feel good. You get a dopamine hit because, as we know, it's better to give than receive. You affirm you have value. You validate your expertise in this topic area. Your inner critic is silenced by the thankfulness of the networking members. The networking leader is thrilled and is more aware of your awesomeness. She'll refer prospective clients to you in the future because she trusts you'll help. Other attendees see you as 'a super problem-solver.' It's a win-win-win for everyone!

We can thank our strong, passionate Spring selves for writing such an awesome Manifesto, a truly empowering guiding document for us to use for decisions that are authentic and true-to-our-best-selves when we stand at our Crossroads.

Affirmation + Action = Your Secret Sauce to Success.

There is More Than One Way to Manifesto

Your Manifesto can help you harness your business brilliance in other ways, too.

One year I created a new Micro-Manifesto every month based on a different theme, such as:

January—content creation
February—financials
March—marketing
April—visibility
May—sales
June—customer journey

Each month, I wrote 5-8 actionable items on the theme and expanded on them in my journal. In January, for example, one item was: *Share your ideas.*

For my journal entry, I wrote:

> *"When I feel inspired about something I want to share, I will record a video, write a post, send an email, or put up an image on social media so the message can reach the people who need it."*

As the year went on, my wall became my super-specific-support-central, helping me to move forward through Spring and onto Summer in my business.

There were times I had new ideas come to me and I just added them to printouts hanging on my wall. They were an ever-growing, ever-evolving tool for my focus and empowerment.

Another modification is to partner your powerful words with images to create an action-packed Vision Board. This understated tool holds a lot of power. The idea is to create a collage of images and words that set the vision for your future. To really activate the power, make it real. Instead of adding a generic bakery photo to your board, find a picture of your dream storefront and then add a picture of you and your store name over the door. See it, feel it, activate it, and your conscious and subconscious will work to make it real.

What if you want to write a book? How would you blend powerful words with images for your Vision Board? Instead of cutting out this week's Bestseller List from your newspaper and pretending you are on it, take it to the next level. Go into a design program (like Canva for example), design an image that looks like a Bestseller List placing YOUR book title in the number one spot. You could also add a small *Featured Author* box on the side of the bestseller list, and place a picture of you, smiling and holding YOUR book. Every time you see your Vision Board, you will absorb the image of your name and your book being at the top of the Bestseller List, and your subconscious mind will guide you to take action towards making that a reality.

10. Bliss List

"To be happy-one must find one's bliss."

~ ***Gloria Vanderbilt***

Bliss is defined as a state of *perfect happiness.* The pinnacle of joy. When we're in bliss, we feel our best, like how we feel on a perfect Summer day (which after doing so much Internal Spring Cleaning, is the season right around the corner). What is on your bliss list?

We're going to use our senses to create a Bliss List.

I know you would have no problems filling this chart out for your personal life (your kid's laughter, your favorite fuzzy socks, grandma's apple pie), but I ask you to fill this out for your business life. Trust me, it will be harder! Whenever you feel yourself sliding towards Winter, refer to your Bliss List and anchor yourself back in Spring. Some ideas include:

- Holding your published book for the first time.
- Looking out at the audience before your speech.
- Seeing your growing bank account after a sale.
- The moment you won a lucrative contract.

Sight	Sound	Smell	Taste	Touch	Memories

"Accentuate the joy of your heart, experiencing a life of bliss."

~ Steven Redhead, Author

As you gain new professional experiences, remember to add them to your Bliss List so it stays current and relevant. This chart is a great resource for when you're at the Crossroads and want to get to Summer but you need a little inspiration to get there.

Post-Internal Spring Cleaning

How are you feeling after this massive Internal Spring Cleaning? Can you see why I recommended selecting a few strategies this time around, and then leave the rest for later? This could be the deepest deep cleaning you have ever done on your mindset.

Do you feel sparkly and shiny? HA! I hear you snickering. Most likely, you feel raw, vulnerable, and an totally overwhelmed! That's totally normal.

Remember that huge rock in the yard you wanted to move? Well, through these ten Spring Cleaning strategies, we have moved the rock. And guess what's under the rock? It isn't sugar and spice and everything nice—it's more dirt, heaps of creepy crawly bugs, maybe some weeds, and many smaller rocks.

Great things take time, my eager entrepreneur.

Yes, it's more fun to buy the sofa and hang the curtains, but when you're building a house, you don't start with décor, you start with ensuring you have a solid foundation. That's what we did inside our mindset— we're ensuring we have a solid foundation.

Now it's time to jump into the next level of Spring Cleaning-the tasks that live outside of our minds.

External Spring Cleaning

Once we've completed a thorough cleaning of our habits, practices, and behaviors, once we've worked through some of the exercises, and once we've recovered from the heavy emotional lifting, we're ready to move onto how we show up in the world.

External Spring Cleaning helps our public facing self. Five categories outside of our mindset to examine are:

1. *Where* Your Magic Happens
2. CEO Meetings
3. Your A-Team
4. Your Back End
5. Your C-Side

1. *Where Your Magic Happens*

You didn't know we would actually clean, did you?

Clutter is often referred to as *stagnant energy*, and it's both draining and overwhelming to those living or working in it. Physical clutter creates mental clutter. The overwhelming amount of papers, books, junk mail, sample products, forms, kid art and other things we pile around us blocks the flow of ideas and creativity. Plus, it wastes precious time as we shuffle things around to find what we're looking for.

Cleaning our physical workspace helps us because:

1. We'll be more efficient because we'll know where things are when we need them, ie a bill, an order.
2. It helps our mental health. Research shows depression can manifest in severe disorganization.
3. Clutter is distracting. When we move things around, we unearth things we'd forgotten about and it derails our focus, whether it was important (like an unpaid bill) or not-important (like an old catalogue of dreamy home décor). We're off task.
4. We aren't overloading our brain. Clutter forces our brain to divide its power between the task we're doing and all the undone tasks around us.
5. De-cluttering your digital space is as important as your physical space — they both overload your brain. Delete/archive things no longer needed.

It's possible to go too far and declutter to the point of extreme minimalism—I don't advocate for that! One study on workplace management and productivity strategies showed that a bare desk, or a stark work environment, removed a person's sense of identity and actually reduced work and quality of that work.

The same research showed people thrived with an organized workspace surrounded by plants and art. Don't just put up any art, though. In the space where you do most of your work, hang *your* art: your vision board, your powerful Manifesto printed on nice paper, photos from past events, cards from clients, your annual goals, testimonials and mementos.

Once the clutter is under control, assess your workspace. Do you have what you need to do your work? What could you add to your space to support and enhance your business brilliance?

"Get rid of clutter and you may just find that it's
been blocking the door you've been looking for."
~ **Katrina Mayer, Author**

2. CEO Meetings

Without question, this is one of the most powerful Spring Cleaning practices you can adopt. It helps you step out of the day-to-day business activities and see how you're really doing as an entrepreneur.

Think about if you are driving to a new destination, really far away, and you never checked your map! How would you know if that turn four hours ago was the correct turn? CEO meetings keep your finger on the pulse of your business and help you prioritize your workload, organize your schedule, track your key metrics, and explore new opportunities. If changes need to be made, they can be made now, not in two months' time when it will be much harder.

This is not time for you to work IN your business. This is time for you to work ON your business.

Oh, wait. What's the difference, you ask? Working IN your business (80-90% of your time) is when you:

- *Do your business,* such as making the products you sell, creating content you provide, meeting with your clients, selling your services, speaking at conferences – whatever you sell.

- Meet partners, investors, vendors, or suppliers
- Implement your offerings for clients such as building webpages, writing reports, etc.
- Answer queries for potential clients
- Send invoices, manage appointments

Working ON your business (spend 10-20% time here during your CEO Meeting) is when you:

- Increase skills/knowledge (reading, learning).
- Create systems to improve efficiency.
- Set goals and plan for the future.
- Measure success—based on how you define it.
- Automate processes.
- Design ways to strengthen your brand (new marketing strategy, a new promotion)
- Write content blogs/articles/tips about your industry or market trends
- Talk with mentors, mastermind groups.
- Explore partnerships for collaboration.

Another power move for your CEO time is to reflect on the past 30/60/90 days and see what has been working. What needs an infusion of your time/ money/energy next week? What no longer serves you? What needs to be refreshed, reorganized, or replaced?

It's said that entrepreneurs are willing to work eighty hours a week for themselves to avoid working forty hours a week for someone else. During our time, it's critical to analyze the bigger picture: what we're creating, where we may need support, and how we should spend our time next week. When we CEO well, we move through Spring toward Summer and be firmly planted in our business brilliance.

Work IN your business = doing your business.
Work ON your business = focus on CEO level tasks.

3. *Your A-Team*

> *"In the right formation, the lifting power of many wings can achieve twice the distance of any bird flying alone."*
>
> **~Author Unknown**

Motivational speaker Jim Rohn famously said we are the average of the five people we spend the most time with. If the five people you spend the most time with are the ones who fan the flames of doubt, fear, or criticism, you need to change things fast.

Particularly when we're new to our business, the people we've always hung around don't really get the entrepreneurial journey: the frenetic ups and downs, the relentless workload, the long hours, the stress. They tell us to go back to our old jobs. They suggest we aren't cut out for owning our own business. It's not about how much we love them or how much they love us, it's about change, and people often resist change.

Typically, friendships and relationships transform (or end) when someone becomes an entrepreneur. There are just too many drastic changes for people to accept. If you have people in your life constantly telling you to quit, or throw in the towel, they're not your people! You'll need new people in your life asap!

Spring Cleaning your relationships will leave you with an epic and supportive A-Team, or advisory team, and will allow you to tap into the best skills of those around you so you can be in your business brilliance.

> *"Behind every successful woman is a tribe of other successful women who have her back."*
>
> *~ **Author Unknown***

Here are some A-Team relationships to consider:

1. **Panel of Advisors**: This team meets with you as a group (in-person or online) to offer feedback and guidance for your big-picture goals. They may provide overall strategies or industry connections. If there's a financial component to this relationship, it's a percentage of future earnings, not an hourly rate.

2. **Mentor:** This person is experienced in business and can give feedback on your ideas or share stories from their entrepreneurial journey. Historically, there haven't been financial components to this relationship, but lately, more people are hiring and paying mentors.

3. **Business Coach**: This person supports you on a portion of your self-discovery journey. Coaches are not

consultants (they don't tell you what to do) or therapists (they don't dive into your past.) They help with performance, ask you questions to stimulate solutions, and hold you accountable to your goals.

4. **Mastermind Group:** This group is designed to be an equal-opportunity experience for all members. Using the power of everyone's experience and knowledge to brainstorm solutions, businesses grow and develop much faster than businesses without this level of collective support. There are some free mastermind groups, but the turnover tends to be high and the quality of support may be lacking. Often, the most successful masterminds are typically paid.

5. **Networking Group**: Every metropolitan area has many different types of networking groups which provide community, education, and information. Networking groups cover the spectrum, from super general (you have a business, come join us) to super specific (you make crafts and have sold in at least three fairs, come join us). Each group has its own style and focus so explore your area to find a good fit.

6. **Accountability Partner**: Best for two or three people max. Each person focuses on one business for a set period of time, then you switch to the other business. If we stumble, they help us reframe limiting beliefs, analyze our challenges, explore other options, and set

new goals. We're much more likely to act if someone is paying attention, and we're more likely to stay in Spring if we have someone to by our side. Some things to consider for accountability partners:

- The meeting style: When? Where? How often? How long per person? How long is the session?
- Decide if you will do round-robin-style of 'anyone can speak at any time' or have a set order to talk.
- How you want to be challenged. Gently? Firmly?
- How many goals to set before the next session?
- Hold a session and test. Any tweaks needed?

How you design your A-Team is up to you, just don't entrepreneur alone! When we isolate ourselves from our colleagues, we tend to see things that aren't there (like our raging fears), we don't see things that are right in front of us (we spotlight because we're riddled with self-doubt) and we create stories for why things aren't working in our business (limiting beliefs).

When you need a hand, reach out for one. When you are firmly planted in Summer, you can reach out and lift up someone else in need. Sometimes that's through sharing knowledge, sometimes that's sharing their business to your friends, sometimes that's helping them take off their mask of perfection or fear.

As we will soon discover though, we're really good at hiding the things we don't want others to see.

"When a flower doesn't bloom, you fix the environment in which it grows, not the flower."

~ Alexander Den Heijer,
Inspirational Speaker

4. Your Back End

When you are in Spring Cleaning mode in your house, it's tempting to skip over *that* drawer, or *that* closet because it's just so overwhelming. Your denial doesn't make it go away, it just delays the inevitable.

That's how many entrepreneurs feel about Spring Cleaning their back end. When I looked online to find a good definition for *back end,* the first entry was from the Oxford Dictionary. It stated: *being farthest away from the front end.* That's actually perfect!

Our front end is what we do for our clients. It's what we do as our business. Our back end is all the stuff we shove away and pray it never needs any attention. In my coaching, entrepreneurs typically push three things away: finances, legal, and tech.

How does the back end impact our business brilliance? When we ignore or poorly manage our finances, our legal obligations or our tech needs, we can't reach our full potential. We might unleash a barrage of ANTs (automatic negative thoughts) to blame for our lack of success, but in reality, we just lost control of our back end. You're amazing at what you do, but if you aren't an expert in finances, legal or tech areas, you need to hire professionals to help you clean up your back end.

One limiting belief I often hear about these key business areas is, "No one is really good at these things." Not true!

Psychologist and author Gay Hendricks wrote a must-read book, *The Big Leap,* and he outlined a framework for happiness and fulfillment in our work, identifying four zones of function:

Zone of Incompetence. Avoid! Others are better at it.
Zone of Competence. You're ok but others are better.
Zone of Excellence. You're higher-skilled than most.
Zone of Genius. Hello brilliance! You're the best at it.

For your success, aim to operate in your zone of genius as often as you can. Also, allow others to be in *their* zone of genius as often as you can, which includes doing all the deep cleaning in the back end categories.

Finances
A study by TD Bank asked over 500 small business owners what they loved and loathed about their business. 96% loved the flexibility and feeling of control, while 58% said bookkeeping was their least favorite task. Managing finances can feel very daunting. Bookstore shelves overflow with how-to guides because it doesn't come natural or easy to many creative entrepreneurs.

When we have this *space of shame* in our business —things we don't look at, stay on top of, or actively manage—we risk falling back into Winter. Either we get into financial hot water or we get stuck in shame because we feel incompetent in our businesses.

Knowing our numbers helps us be capable and confident. With good data, we make good decisions from a place of authority, staying firmly in Spring.

Here are some preliminary questions to help you evaluate if this is an area that needs some cleaning, or if you need a professional team:

How is my profit? How is my cash flow?
Many people use financial terms interchangeably, but here are a few money terms to know:

Revenue is the total income a business earns from normal activities (sales, royalties, commissions).

Expenses are the amounts you must pay to cover taxes, production costs, raw materials, other bills.

Profit, or net income, is the amount you have after all expenses are deducted from your revenue.

Cash flow is the money that's moving, or flowing, in and out of your business each month. If more money is coming in (received from clients) than going out (paying your bills), you have positive cash flow. If you have more money going out than coming in, you have negative cash flow.

a. *Where is my money coming from?*
Explore what products or services bring in most of your income and rank the performance of all your offerings to see what generates the most revenue.

b. *Where is money not coming from? (And is there hope this could change in the future?)*

Look closely at the cost to provide your product or service. Does it cost you more to do it than the income you earn from it? If your offer is under-earning, evaluate if it's a dead-end, or if it has future potential/can drive revenue in other ways.

Natalie is a glass artist and for a long time, she had two product lines. Her biggest inventory was in glass accessories for home décor, like coasters, trays, and serving platters. They were created in a muted palette because she felt that would appeal to more people. Her smaller line was beverage glassware in the Mondrian-style, with bright, bold colors and geometric shapes. Anytime she launched a new glassware design, her clients raced to buy it while her décor sales were flat. And, when we ran the numbers, we found her glassware line was covering the costs to produce her home décor line. Until she looked at her finances, she didn't have any idea her passion project was so lucrative. She held a flash sale of her home décor items and started to focus exclusively on her smaller line. She said goodbye to the 'starving artist' persona and made good money selling her beautiful martini glasses, wine glasses, and decanters.

It was a clear choice for Natalie, but not for Jaycee.

Jaycee is a holistic healer who helps people with overall life balance and aligning the body, mind and soul. Her long-term clients love working with her, but she struggled to build her practice because she lived so far from the city. Every week, she spent hours driving to meet with potential clients. She realized most people had low knowledge about holistic healing and much of her time was in educating them, but not signing them on as clients.

How could she help people understand the possibility of holistic healing without her driving and personally explaining it week after week? After some research, she decided to launch a podcast to share her philosophy and the benefits of holistic healing. She spent hundreds of dollars every month for eleven months without seeing a penny of return, stressing and doubting and worrying about how to cover all these new expenses. However, just before her year anniversary, she signed four new clients and secured three advertisers to serve her growing audience. It took time, but her investment into her podcast did eventually generate revenue for her business.

What can I do about my money situation?
There are two sides to this story.

You can increase revenue. Can you make more of what you make or offer more services? Create VIP options or lucrative packages? Can you upsell current clients?

You can decrease expenses. Can you cut costs, reduce spending, or scale back operations? Can you partner or collaborate to share costs? Can you do more of your business online to cut travel, printing, or rental costs?

Your financial team can advise you on which parts of your financial house need attention, and which would benefit from some investment or divestment.

Legal

This is one area that needs to be intentional, thorough and specific to your business. There is no shortcut. There are limitless legal considerations for your specific business you need to know because neglecting this area could unleash a personal or professional blizzard if you aren't legally protected. Here are some topics to consider with a professional:

- Legal business structures.
- Local, state, federal government requirements.
- Your rights/responsibilities to clients/investors.
- Raising capital without breaking SEC regulations.
- Intellectual property patent/trademark/copyright.
- Privacy rights and security.
- Email list opt-ins and online terms of service.
- Partnership agreements.
- Hiring: independent contractors vs. employees.
- Licensing and permits.
- Liability and insurance.
- Disputes, mediation, lawsuits.
- Contracts with everyone about everything.

You may know a lovely lawyer up the road, but don't put yourself through the Winter stress of hiring the wrong lawyer. Ask your networking groups for referrals to someone specializing in small business entities to protect you and your business.

Technology

Many entrepreneurs have a love/hate relationship with technology. When it works seamlessly and predictably, they love it.

When it crashes, disconnects, or doesn't behave as expected, the frustration sends us into immediate Winter.

First, consider your skill and interest in mastering your tech. Some entrepreneurs use only a few tech items and that is all they need. Yay! Others have many systems we count on to run our businesses, such as:

- Your computer and hi-speed internet access.
- Software to run your business (calendar, word processing, spreadsheets, design programs).
- Online orders/In person orders.
- Inventory, fulfillment, delivery or shipping.
- Invoicing and billing management.
- Website management—updating and content
- Email and digital newsletters (our mailing lists)
- Online privacy and security.

There are incredible technology professionals whose expertise is being your technology consultant. They help with implementing solutions, trouble-shooting, or mapping out your whole technology infrastructure to ensure your system is optimized.

Find them. Hire them. Stay in your zone of genius.

5. Your C-Side

C stands for clients. This is where the rubber hits the road in your business. Are you creating a product that people want to buy? Are you solving a problem that people will pay for?

When we're Spring Cleaning our C-Side, let's confirm who we think our clients are *actually* matches who our clients are.

Your Ideal Client

Who buys from you? Consider data from:

- Buyer information from a registration form.
- Information from your social media groups.
- Anecdotal information you find online.
- After-purchase testimonials or reviews.
- Referrals.

If you're struggling in your business and can't find your brilliance, it may be that you aren't targeting the right people with the right message in the right way.

You wouldn't be the first.

David H. McConnell was born in Oswego N.Y. in 1858. He grew up watching his father run the family farm and manufacture bricks. He wanted something different. When he turned twenty-one, he went to New York City and got a job selling books door-to-door.

Sales were low. He struggled. If he stopped there, he may have ended his short-lived career thinking he was a terrible salesman, or that he had an inferior product, or he wasn't cut out for this kind of work and needed to go back home and work on the farm.

Instead, he thought about his C-Side.

Almost every door McConnell knocked on was opened by a woman. They were home alone, lonely, bored, and isolated from others. He decided he'd give a little gift to the women who bought his books, a small vial of perfume he'd hand-blended on his own time.

Very quickly, women didn't want the books at all, they just wanted the gift. Women wanted perfume.

Once he got clear on what his ideal client wanted, he left the book business. In 1886, he formed his own company. McConnell's business skyrocketed. Now, 133 years later, with annual sales of $5.7 billion worldwide in 2017 and 6.4 million representatives, it's the fifth-largest beauty company and the second largest direct-selling enterprise in the world.

You may not know McConnell's name, but you know his company: Avon.

Now it's your turn. Who is your ideal client? Take as much time as you need to understand your C-Side.

1. What is their age, gender, socioeconomic status? Are they married? Kids? Pets?
2. What do they value?
3. What is their pain?
4. What do they need?
5. How do you solve it?
6. What is their life like after your offering?
7. What would their life be like if they didn't buy it?
8. How do your clients find out about you?
9. Do they prefer online or in person shopping?
10. Where online do they spend time? Facebook? YouTube? Instagram? Pinterest? LinkedIn?
11. How do they actually purchase your offering? (Cash, Credit, PayPal?)
12. How do they receive your offering? (Digital? Shipped? In person?)

13. Is it a one-time transaction or do you/can you create a relationship?
14. What may prevent your ideal client from purchasing from you?
15. What other options exist to solve their problem/meet their need?

You don't have to know everything about your client right away, but if you think your ideal client is *everybody*, you've got work to do.

Even if you create a product everyone uses, like toilet paper, you don't actually sell it to everyone — you sell to the shopper who stands in the aisle and selects your brand over other brands around them. Next time you're at a grocery store, try to determine the ideal client that different brands target. It's fun!

Jemma loved helping people and left her human resources job to pursue a certificate in life coaching. She loved the self-discovery that came through her training. She loved how her clients praised her compassion and guidance. Even if they weren't a good fit, Jemma signed them up, sometimes sacrificing her own values to support their transformation.

When any client needed her, day or night, she always emailed, called, and texted back right away because, well, they needed her. She felt crushed when they hit setbacks and felt elated when they succeeded.

Then changes started to appear.

She mindlessly added more junk food to her cart at the grocery store. She drank more coffee than usual, disturbing her thinking and sleeping. She was annoyed by her dogs and snapped at her dad when he suggested she take a break from her heavy schedule.

"I need to do this because this is what it takes to be a good life coach. Don't you realize they need me? They can't do anything without me!"

The words hung in the air like frozen breath on a dark winter night. Jemma didn't have an overloaded schedule problem, she had a boundary problem. Let's explore boundaries.

> *"We need to have a talk on the subject of what's yours and what's mine."*
>
> **~ From the book,**
> **The Girl with the Dragon Tattoo**

Setting and Upholding Firm Boundaries

We hear a lot about setting personal boundaries, but setting professional boundaries are just as critical.

Through boundaries, we teach people how to treat us. It's important that we choose what we want in our business relationships, and then teach our clients, investors, and employees how to be in a business relationship with us. But knowing we teach our clients how to treat us isn't enough.

Jemma taught her clients how to treat her: emails, calls and texts at any time of the day or night were all fine. Eventually Jemma would've felt suffocated by the endless demands on her time and energy.

The risk here is she may have created a story that she wasn't a good life coach because she was feeling resentful or bothered. Or she could've fallen into Winter and succumbed to her negative thoughts about how she can't handle her new business venture. Neither of these would be true, because her struggles weren't about her abilities or talents at all, but about the loose boundaries she set with her clients.

There are many ways our businesses will test our self-worth and keep us teetering on the edge between Spring and Winter. It isn't about how much we love our businesses or if our clients are ideal or not. It's about how we provide our expertise without a high personal cost. It's about boundaries.

What are Boundaries?

Boundaries are emotional or physical limits we set to communicate our values by sharing how we want to be treated, what we will accept, what we will tolerate, and what's not welcome. These are especially critical for entrepreneurs who work from home because the lines between home life and work are easily blurred.

Examples of weak business boundaries include:

- Responding to every call, text, or email right away.
- Constantly canceling plans to meet client needs.
- Accepting any behavior.
- Saying yes whether we want to or not.
- Committing but feeling procrastination or dread.

To be in Spring, we need to have stronger boundaries that protect our time, energy, and resources. If there is someone or something in your business encroaching too deeply, let's re-establish firmer boundaries. We can start with one small boundary and use the process below:

1. Identify a time you felt disempowered or resentful.
2. Create a new rule to honor your values and needs.
3. Describe your expectations and desired outcomes.
4. Share it with all people involved in that situation (clients, partners, staff, vendors).
5. Respect the rule and enforce it consistently.

This Spring Cleaning activity may be more challenging for creative entrepreneurs or those who derive great value from helping other people.

However, when your clients or employees see your boundaries are more like swinging saloon doors and less like bank vault doors, their behavior impacts you negatively. You'll work twice as hard to stay in Spring because your soft boundaries will keep you on Winter's doorstep and in a state of chaos.

If we struggle with soft boundaries, we may see:

1. One or two clients always pushing the limits.
2. Many clients overstepping the same limits.

If it's the first case, why do these few clients cause you to abandon your boundaries? Do they remind you of someone else you feel indebted to? What's beneath your emotional attachment to them or their success?

If it's the second case, what keeps you afraid of putting your foot down? The answer here is often payment. Entrepreneurs aren't comfortable asking for money, so invoices linger, putting stress on you and your business. Even if it isn't money, if it's impacting your work, stress, or time, it needs to be handled.

Boundaries are a bit like gravity; you can't see it, but you can see the effects. Jemma didn't know she had boundary issues, but her father saw the effects. Here are things you can look out for in your own life:

- You become more easily overwhelmed.
- You struggle at the Crossroads with decisions.
- You feel heaviness when someone faces a setback.
- You start seeking more approval.
- You blur where you end and someone else begins.
- You say yes more than you want.
- You feel anxious in interactions.
- You experience negative thoughts more than usual.
- You neglect self-care to free yourself up.
- You feel taken advantage of.
- You feel chronically agitated.
- You start to feel bitter or resentful.
- You fear your boundaries will lead to rejection.

When our boundaries are too wishy-washy, Winter is right around the corner. Let's look at some common boundary issues, and ways to resolve them.

Issue: Unreasonable Expectations
Why you've tolerated it: You're afraid of rejection. You don't want to offend them or risk losing business.

What does it look like in your business? You don't have detailed contracts or agreements. You can't remember what you promised. What they want makes sense, so you should just do the work, even though you do it with some resentment.

New Boundary: Write very detailed contracts for your offerings. Read your proposals and contracts carefully to ensure clarity on what you provide.

Issue: Scope Creep For Free (Your clients keep modifying existing projects/add more items as the project proceeds. You don't bill for extra work)
Why you've tolerated it: You have money mindset issues; you're afraid of being called greedy or money-hungry if you keep increasing your rates.

What does it look like in your business? Surely you can build a few more webpages, bake a few more cupcakes, or give a few more hours of help because you like to make your clients happy.

New Boundary: Prevent scope creep by leaving no wiggle room in your contract. Detail everything.

Every contract should include a comprehensive checklist of work to be completed, along with a timeline for the project, and the total to be paid (plus all your other legally required contract components).

Every contract should also include a second form called a *Proposal For Contract Addendum Form* which is to be filled out if any requests come up outside of the original agreement. Some entrepreneurs list their hourly rate on this contract to make it clear that all changes have cost implications. Specify the rate is *to be determined based on the time and resources required.*

If a client reaches out for any changes, you can be excited to hear more, then let them know you will send out the *Proposal For Contract Addendum Form* to really understand their needs. Some clients may be surprised or upset, especially if you always bit your tongue and did the work.

If that happens, mention that you were finding that you couldn't provide the level of incredible service you wanted to provide when clients made ongoing changes. This form gives you clarity and sets expectations so you can continue to do your best.

When you receive their form, you'll evaluate the work and send back a Contract Addendum with the additional work, new timeline, and estimated cost. Setting a scope-creep boundary protects your time and energy, and ensures you can meet their needs with the level of quality you want to provide.

Issue: Billing disputes.
Why you've tolerated it: Discussing money is hard.

What does it look like in your business? If a client disputes the bill, you reduce it to stop the awkward feelings. If you charge by the hour, perhaps it makes you feel slow, or not worth the amount you charged.

New Boundary: If you have an hourly model, your intake form lists many questions about the project so you can provide an accurate estimate of the cost.

If you can offer alternatives, consider a flat-fee for an agreed-upon project. This prevents cost surprises for your client at the end of the contract. Be aware of scope-creep here and put everything in writing. This model requires time-management testing on your end – how fast you work, what things take longer, and what components of the job are time-hogs.

If it's a bigger project, or takes place over a longer period, pre-determine milestones. You provide updates to the client on project progress and let them know how much more you still need to complete.

Issue: Unpaid bills
Why you've tolerated it: You don't trust your worth.

What does it look like in your business? You resist asking for payment because you don't have a strong system to secure payments. You hate to harass people for money. This issue is ripe for creating stories about why a bill wasn't paid. For example:

- "They'll pay when they can, I trust them."
- "They probably paid their important bills first."
- "They aren't happy with how long it took."
- "They are dissatisfied with the final product."

New Boundary: Payment is required at the time the contract is signed by both parties.

Many long-time entrepreneurs share stories of doing the work and being paid on-time without struggle when they started out decades ago, but they say that's not the case anymore. Today, it's important to build the payment terms into every agreement. Consider requiring a large portion before the project starts and the final balance upon completion.

Another item to establish is the process if there is dissatisfaction. Is there a money back guarantee or is it a final sale? Is there a 30-day return policy on unused items? Is there a re-stocking fee? The rise of online shopping has created so many new considerations for entrepreneurs as they work with their clients.

The relationship with your C-Team is crucial for your business brilliance to shine, but you can't give so much away that there's nothing left for you. Every time you say yes to one person, or one project, or one commitment, you are saying no to something else. Maybe you are saying no to time with your family, or time to create new programs or courses, or time to do things in your own life.

Success in Spring

Spring is a powerful season full of possibility and hope. Success in Spring is not about making everything different or becoming a totally new entrepreneur. It's about finding what works for you and your business ... and doing more of it.

When you honor yourself and your needs in your business, you will most certainly flow right into Summer.

"And so with the sunshine and the great bursts of leaves growing on the trees, just as things grow in fast movies, I had that familiar conviction that life was beginning over again with the summer."

~ F. Scott Fitzgerald, Author

CHAPTER 4

Summer

There is no denying the sweetness of this season. Fruits and veggies, at the peak of ripeness, are juicy and full of flavor. The sun shines brilliantly. We're happy, feeling strong and empowered. We enjoy the longest days and the shortest nights, allowing plenty of time to be mentally, physically, and emotionally full of joy and good energy. We kind of sparkle.

Contentment and confidence reigns during the Summer— we finally have time to be in our zone of genius for longer periods of time. We enjoy creating new solutions or new partnerships. We play, explore, and simply thrive in our bright, beautiful world.

What is Summer?

Being in Summer is what we crave. It brings a peace and joy that feels like the bright sun warming us to our core. It's our happy place! It's where we go to draw deep inner peace, strength, and profound nourishment to our life, our relationships, and our passions. When we're in Summer, we feel:

- Happy to be working in our business
- Excited for what we're creating
- Open to learning new things to grow

- Forgiving of small mistakes
- Emotionally present in our interactions
- Feeling sure we can overcome anything
- A vibrant, positive energy in our mood
- Confident, capable, connected to our best selves

Ask any entrepreneur in Summer and she'll be the first to say while it is glorious, it doesn't happen by accident. You invest, nurture and cultivate your business brilliance so you can enjoy the Summer days.

Remember, it may not have been that long ago when you felt stuck in your stormy Winter. You worked really hard to Spring Clean and now is the time to blossom with new growth and possibility.

Once you arrive in Summer, you'll have to work to stay here, running your business with purpose to stay in heart-centered connection with your goals. When you're more mindful of ways you slide into Winter, you'll intentionally choose ways to cultivate your self-awareness, confidence, and courage to prevent returning to the dark season.

Think about it like this: You'd like to grow veggies.

You buy the soil and the seeds. Is that all it takes to grow food? Of course not, that's only one step! You work hard to break up the hard soil, preparing it to nourish the seeds. Is that enough? Well, *something* might grow, but likely only a small percentage of what *could* grow if you tended diligently to your garden.

It takes clearing, tilling, regular watering, weeding, mulching, protecting your garden from pests and other creatures, maybe even extra nutrients to help it reach its full potential. Creating a healthy and vibrant garden takes time and investment and constant care.

The same is true for nurturing a healthy and vibrant entrepreneur - so much goes into your success.

Common Traits of Entrepreneurs in Summer

- We think positively. A lot.
- We're our biggest cheerleader, which means we control when and how we get back to Summer.
- We don't wait to be rescued.
- We expand our thinking, grow our awareness, and commit to trying new things.
- We honor our core values and beliefs.
- We constantly challenge stories of shame or unworthiness, forgiving as needed.
- We're okay with feeling vulnerable.
- We accept that adversity, disagreements, and frustrations are natural parts of fully living.
- We find the best solutions for the situation.

Notice making oodles of money isn't on the list. We want to make great money, but we crave freedom, control, autonomy, flexibility, and influence more. And, we endure stress, sacrifice and long hours to get it.

Why do we risk so much for a chance to feel brilliant? Strategy consultant Jon Burgstone said this:

"Entrepreneurship isn't simply about launching new ventures or making money. Instead, it's about solving problems and creating social progress; building great new things that make a better world. It's about celebrating each step toward the ultimate human longing for an enhanced and enriched enterprise of life... It's the creative process itself, with a focus on meaningful problem solving, that leads people to deeper levels of consciousness and truer truths."

And happiness.

Summer (to most of us) is a life of fulfilment, meaning, and happiness. Some people say being an entrepreneur has nothing to do with being happy, but I disagree. We become entrepreneurs because most traditional jobs stifle our creative thinking and deny any hope for flexibility and human design. We leave corporate work because we want to create meaning and change the world. We wouldn't work this hard, risk this much, or push this relentlessly if we didn't experience Summer happiness on our journey.

However, happiness isn't just about smiles and giggles so let's see what it really means.

Happiness

Psychology Today Online published a set of articles about happiness and this was the introduction:

"Ah, happiness, that elusive state. Philosophers, theologians, psychologists, and even economists have long sought to define it, and since the 1990s, a whole branch of psychology—positive psychology—has been dedicated to pinning it down and propagating it. More than simply positive mood, happiness is a state of well-being that encompasses living a good life—that is, with a sense of meaning and deep satisfaction.

Much has been written about happiness and entire organizations just research the science of happiness.

According to Dr. Emiliana Simon-Thomas, director at The Greater Good Science Center at the University of California, Berkeley, happiness is "the propensity to feel positive emotions, the capacity to recover from negative emotions quickly, and holding a sense of purpose. Happiness is not having a lot of privilege or money. It's not constant pleasure. It's a broader thing: Our ability to connect with others, to have meaningful relationships, to have a community."

Happiness is when life fulfills most of your needs and many of your wants. As entrepreneurs, we find happiness from solving problems, building something, nurturing relationships, and finding meaning or purpose in our work. It's refreshing to hear happiness isn't smiling every second with no negative feelings intruding on your cheerful life.

Not even close!

The science of happiness discovered happy people have negative things happen all the time, but it doesn't knock them down or push them into Winter.

Why is that?

Because happiness is a mindset that helps you rate your life as *mostly good*.

When we train ourselves to see life as mostly good, it doesn't mean everything is perfect. It means we feel confident we can create good things in our life. We know we control our responses and reactions. In the face of a challenge or difficult situation, we know we have everything we need to get through it and come out stronger, wiser, and more resilient. That process helps strengthen our happiness muscle.

Some of us might think that we don't have that kind of power. Maybe you're a *glass half empty* person. Maybe your parents are pessimists so you feel that is your destiny, too. Or happiness is out of reach because of the shame you carry or the scars you hide.

If we were in a car, sitting side by side, I'd stop the car right here. I would turn to you and look into your beautiful eyes and tell you the absolute truth:

You are worthy of happiness because you are you.

You don't need to earn it, justify it, or barter for it.

If this makes you uncomfortable, or if you scoffed, I'll say it again—*you are absolutely worthy of happiness without doing anything. All you need to do is choose it.*

Summer welcomes everyone, genetics, scars and all.

When you believe you can choose happiness, you change your outlook and your health as well. People who rate themselves as 'happy' experience:

- Lower heart rate and blood pressure.
- Lower risk for heart disease.
- A stronger immune system.
- Fewer pains with chronic disease.

Knowing what makes us happy is where it all begins. I've included some questions below to help you harness your happiness, but you can also refer to your *Bliss List* from Spring if you need a little guidance.

When you read the following questions, your first responses will likely be personal. That's natural! You can make two lists: personal and professional.

1. What makes you the happiest?
2. What memories bring you the greatest joy?
3. How can you experience happiness right now?
4. Do you have the power to bring more happiness to your life, or do you feel like it's out of your control?

The Happiness You Can Control

While some people think they have limited control over their happiness, that isn't what science shows.

Happiness expert Sonja Lyubomirsky, Ph.D. authored the bestseller *The How of Happiness: A Scientific Approach to Getting the Life You Want* shares that 40% of our happiness comes from what we do and how we think, 10% comes from external factors (finances, career, health, climate, etc.), and 50% comes from our genetically natural temperament. According to Dr. Lyubomirsky, we control 40% of our happiness simply by 'being, doing and thinking.'

To be fair, we don't purposefully decide on every thought as it enters our mind. In fact, our subconscious and unconscious mind filters most of our thoughts for us, without us even knowing! We also have a set of core values and beliefs that invisibly shape how we see things and what we believe is true, impacting our decisions and influencing how we navigate life.

Strategies to Stay in Summer

It's critical to arm yourself with ideas and activities that build your resilience muscle and strengthen your confidence. There are limitless ways to cultivate connection and positively influence our mindset, but we'll explore the most common and effective ways to stay in Summer in a list below.

You may read through this list and think there's no way you can stay in a sunny, positive state of mind just by doing these things. I admit there is nothing magical about this list.

Do you know what makes these ideas powerful?

We *can* do them.

Do you know what makes these ideas lose power?

We *don't* do them.

The sections below give you the basis to create a solid Summer foundation. Select one strategy you can implement today, one you can implement tomorrow, and one more you can add by the end of this week.

You'll find when you start to shift, your whole outlook will shift and you'll stay in Summer longer.

Make Your CEO Meetings Non-Negotiable

One of the most aligned Summer strategies is to schedule and hold real CEO meetings with yourself.

First, it ensures you have dedicated time to think about the things that matter in your business and align your time and energy with your upcoming projects.

Second, having this meeting allows you to work on important components of your business that don't get daily attention, like financial reporting, business development, or strategic long-term planning.

My CEO meeting time is Friday morning, 8-11 am. In that time, I review my current week and schedule time to follow up on things undone, I plan my next week, I track data for my milestones and goals, I identify new ideas or professional connections to explore the next week, and I identify areas of content I can create in my next creation time block. A colleague actually schedules Friday Fun Time after her CEO meeting to celebrate her wins. That's powerful!

Explore Your Creativity

Those of us who stay in Summer tap into our creative flow. It may be doing something that provides space for our creative thoughts to appear (gardening, hiking or making art, when our mind can wander and explore). It may be mind-mapping/ brainstorming new project ideas in a creative way (if you always make lists, try doing it in a more visual way). If you often work alone, try brainstorming with someone else. Staying in Summer means trying things in new ways.

Establish a Meaningful Reward System

All work and no play puts entrepreneurs at risk for burn-out and the return of Winter feelings.

When you have a reward system that works for you, the right motivation is always at your fingertips. This goes to the heart of why you do what you do, why you make the sacrifices you make, and invest as much as you do. Because how you reward yourself is relevant, meaningful and fulfilling. You can refer back to your Define Success exercise we completed earlier to make sure your reward system aligns with you.

Nurture Core Relationships

When you're in Winter, your visibility is low and you can only see what's right in front of you. When you're in Spring, you're busy clearing, recovering, releasing, and creating new, healthy connections to hope, happiness, confidence, and courage. Summer is the time to look around and connect (or reconnect) to core relationships that may have been neglected.

Do you have a mentor? A business networking group? An accountability partner you call every week to encourage and support A book club or fitness group or mastermind cohort?

Science shows that successful leaders always develop key relationships in the good times so they have them in place when the weather turns stormy. In Summer, identify key people who you would like to deepen your business relationship with and invest in them. Allow them to invest in you. It's a win-win.

Honor Your Self-Care Priorities

One of the first items we tackled in our Spring Cleaning section was self-care. Let's face it, your entire business depends on your mental, emotional, physical, and intellectual well-being.

Many entrepreneurs work diligently on their self-care when they're coming out of Winter. As they start to feel, do, and be better, self-care slides off the list.

Business owners who stay in Summer longer know daily self-care is mandatory. Occasional self-care, or emergency self-care, doesn't cut it.

Recommit to the self-care strategies that help you feel your best, do your best, and be your best. Schedule them into your calendar. Honor them. Honor you.

Be at Peace With Your Happymess

Summer isn't about perfection. Happiness isn't deliriously giggling all the time. Staying firmly planted in Summer means we need to accept of what is called our Happymess. When you reduce your expectations, you release your tight grip on the outcome of a situation, and you can just...be okay. It may be a mess, as you describe it, but it's *your* Happymess.

You will be okay.

There is a little something we forget about on our entrepreneurial journey— we have influence and impact, whether we realize it or not. When we do something, anything, we send our energy and wisdom into the world and we just don't know how far the ripples will go. We forget that we change lives just by being us, doing our thing, and taking one step at a time. What we think is messy is a lifeline to someone else. Clients don't come because we're perfect, they come because we are who we are. When we shine in our business brilliance, we inspire other entrepreneurs to shine too. That's a superpower!

When I reflect on my best Summer days in my business, I see that I'm able to give my passion, my solutions, and my ideas to make my client's lives richer. In turn they encourage me, believe in me, and feel gratitude that I created something that changed everything for them. There is a give and a receive and it's in beautiful balance.

The 5 Seasons of Connection was created to check in with ourselves and our mindset as we travel on our entrepreneurial journey. It allows us to understand our darkness, sadness, fears, and doubts, while teaching us that our set point is movable. We can be as confident, determined, and proactive as we want to be. When we always keep in mind that we are taking someone's struggles away, or solving a problem for someone else, it reminds us that we're serving others. No matter what business you have, what product or service you offer, what problem you solve, what you use to do it — you are in the people business. Keeping your eye on the people you serve can keep you feeling the Summer sunshine a lot longer.

And, then life happens.

As much as we want to stay in Summer, inevitably a thick cloud moves in front of the sun, dark shadows fill the sky, and the breeze shifts to a chilly blast.

That, my friend, is the season of Fall creeping in.

We need to take swift and decisive action to pull ourselves back from the brink of disconnection from our business brilliance. If we can't/won't/don't, an unwelcomed chill in the air signals we're sliding into the next season.

> *"Summertime is always the best of what might be."*
>
> *~ Charles Bowden,*
> *Author and Journalist*

CHAPTER 5

Fall

Fall *is a time* when the earth tilts away from the sun, resulting in less daylight, cooling temperatures, and dropping leaves. One day you're soaking up the Summer sun, and then the next day you look around and all the leaves are gone!

Similarly, in *The 5 Seasons of Connection*, Fall creeps in. When we feel the chill, we stop and wonder. *Hold on. Where did all the easy, happy times go? It was so great and now they're gone.*

Our businesses can take us to our edge. They push our buttons, test our resolve, and hold up our weaknesses and magnify them.

What is Fall?

Fall happens when something negative or challenging occurs to test, poke, or push us. We may waver in our resolve, question or doubt ourselves, or even entertain the possibility that we suck.

The start of this season looks different for every entrepreneur, but everyone can remember instances when they noticed it. Here are just a few:

- You lovingly create a beautiful bouquet for a special event. The client looks at it and barely half-smiles when you present it.
- Your client places a last-second order. You squeeze it in, make the product, battle wind and rain to deliver it,

and when you arrive, he sharply asks why did it take so long?

- You worked overtime to meet an early website launch date and when you present the bill, they scoff, and their energy shifts noticeably.

Some would say it's inevitable that our businesses are always in Fall because there are so many moving parts, so many ups and downs, unknowns and unexpected things. It's true, there are many moving parts and ups and downs, but none of those things bring us into Fall alone. *It's the fiery combination of an action and our reaction.*

We don't just *fall* into Fall—we get there because the bountiful Summer garden was neglected and weeds are choking the once-abundant growth.

When life gets busy or chaotic, we may neglect our business brilliance and all we did to reach Summer. We leave ourselves vulnerable to the onset of Fall.

When we head towards Fall, we feel:

- Hurt by something a client says/doesn't say.
- Stretched a bit too thin and fraying at the ends.
- Underappreciated or devalued.
- Like we're a worker, not a partner on a project.
- Stung by a negative review or rating.
- Underrecognized for our contributions.
- Impatient with a client for any reason.

There is often a slice of overextension in Fall. If you are giving too much and receiving too little, the balance is off and you may descend into dark, stormy times. But Fall doesn't have to be the last stop before a certain Winter. Use it as an indicator that things are changing and our attention is required.

Just like the weeds that popped up in our beautiful Summer garden threaten to damage our harvest, neglecting key Spring Cleaning practices will damage your resolve as a business owner.

Let's check in. Are you coming to your business from a place of your Summer?

Or are you already in Fall?

Quick Life Check-Up

You can't be in your business brilliance when you are stressed, stretched, annoyed, agitated, or feeling unworthy. Let's see where we're right now.

Answer yes or no to the following questions:

Feelings Assessment

Y N   Do you think about how you're unappreciated?

Y N   Do you equate feedback with unworthiness?

Y N   Is resentment building inside of you?

Y N   Are you seeking evidence for your inner critic?

Y N   Do you fill in the gaps with assumptions?

Y N   Are you refraining from giving/receiving?

Y N   Are you fixed on only one outcome?

Y N   Is the grass greener elsewhere?

Physical Assessment

Y N   Are your responses a bit too sharp?

Y N   Shoulders or jaw tight, breathing shallow?

Y N   Are you hungry? Thirsty? Tired? Sick?

Y N   Are you cutting out exercise time?

Y N   Are you pushing yourself without sleep?

Y N   Have you felt stress headaches?

Y N   Have you deprioritized outdoor activities?

Y N   Are you surrounded by clutter or chaos?

Emotional Assessment

Y N   Have you neglected your self-care?

Y N   Have you avoided journal writing?

Y N   Have you cancelled plans with friends?

Y N   Do destructive habits help you cope?

Y N   Are you zoning out on TV or social media?

Y N   Have you said yes when you want to say no?

Y N   Do you give with hopes of receiving?

If you answered *yes* to:

 5 or less: You need support for Summer.

 6 or more: You're heading to Fall or there now.

 10 or more: You're heading toward Winter.

Your ability to regulate your reactions is predicated on your current level of self-care. If you haven't been regularly investing in well-being, you're less equipped to bring your confident, capable, powerful self back to Summer.

Once you know where you are, we can find your natural trends and identify your Fall-creating patterns.

How Patterns Push Us To Fall

We're creatures of habit. Most of us live and work in predictable ways. When we take time to break down our patterns, we can identify the unique ways we slide into Fall. Time and time again, we squeeze the water balloon and wonder why we keep getting wet!

Zhanna is a people-pleasing private nurse. Over the past year, she quit four different jobs because she expected to be fired for not getting her work done. Unbeknownst to Zhanna, her Fall-creating pattern emerged in the first conversation with her client —she agreed to do extra time-draining tasks during her shift. As you can surmise, her tasks took longer than expected and Zhanna started to panic. Her ANTs were fierce. "Damn, I keep sucking at this. I need to quit private nursing, I'm too slow and not good enough."

In our session, we identified her Fall-creating patterns and created an action plan to break them.

Your Patterns

Unless we're mindfully dissecting our patterns, we're set to repeat them. We can't just think about them on the surface, we have to examine every action or behavior in our lives and find the deeper meaning and recognize what our patterns are trying to tell us.

Some powerful questions you can ask yourself are:

- What is my role in this situation?
- What lesson can I learn here?
- Has this happened to me before?

- In my past, did I get to the root of the pattern or did I just get through it, ensuring I would repeat it?
- How do I respond differently to break the pattern?
- How do my personal rhythms bring me to Fall?

Personal Rhythms

We often don't think about our personal rhythms in Summer because the flow is smooth and easy. When Fall's chill hits the air, it's time to focus on the ups and downs of our energy, focus, attention, and work speed.

Do we crank out big projects in the morning?
Do we like to connect with others after lunch?
Are our power hours in the afternoon?
Do we do our best work when others go to sleep?
After a big presentation, do we feel energized?

Knowing your personal rhythms will help you plan your day, schedule your meetings, honor your energy, respect your time, and set your boundaries.

In the moment when something threatens to push you into Fall, remember you're feeling something: vulnerable, unappreciated, hurt, afraid, or provoked.

We can't build contingencies against all the challenges in our businesses every day, but the magic of knowing your personal rhythms gives you the opportunity to guide yourself back toward Summer. Feel the Fall feeling, understand it, and release it.

Fall often creeps into our lives like dandelions. One day it's a beautiful green lawn, the next time we look, there's a sea of yellow that wasn't there before. If we look at our current distractions in our businesses, we can see how we missed the weeds that popped up.

What demanded our attention? What consumed us recently? Were we pushing too hard, giving too much, undervaluing our contributions, or denying our awesomeness? Or were we so focused on our giant to-do list that we spotlighted something?

One way we slip into Fall is by allocating our time in ways that leads us toward disconnecting with our business brilliance. Too much busyness or too many soul-draining obligations pull us apart.

Another way we go into Fall is to simply deny ourselves a great Summer experience.

How Do You Dull Your Brilliance?

I was 22 and a student at one of Canada's top journalism programs when I was chosen to create a video to advertise and promote University Housing.

I was on cloud nine! I found a cameraman and we filmed diligently. I wove together a story that evoked laughter, tears, excitement, and hope. It was a hit!

The university thanked me with a VHS copy and a check. I couldn't believe I was paid for doing what I loved so much. I ran across campus to show my video to my favorite journalism professors.

They watched my video, and I watched them, noting every twitch, smile, and eyebrow raise. They were pleased and proud of me, then the lesson came.

One said, "Every year, 300 freshmen arrive in this program and they compete fiercely to earn one of the ninety coveted spots we offer in second year. These kids are hungry for the limelight and national media attention. I can count on one hand how many could show the level of restraint that you demonstrated to make an entire video without leaving any fingerprints.

"On one hand, I applaud you for being professional and not using this to land a job after graduation. On the other hand, where are you? You need to show up. You need to leave your fingerprints on your work. You need to let people know Leanne was here."

We can talk about being brave and wild and free, but in our moments of instinct, we go to what we know. When fear steps in, we unconsciously or subconsciously do the thing we've always done to dull our brilliance or sabotage our growth. Where do you go when you slip into Fall?

Do you hide?
Do you dumb yourself down?
Do you give the first kick when you fall down?
Do you defer to those you hold in higher esteem?
Do you deny who you are in your awesomeness?
Do you rain on your own parade?
Do you buckle down to work harder and longer?

In your business, your habits can be positive, growth-focused, and expansive. Or they can be holding you back, down, and out. Fall can be a gateway to Winter, the door to a darker, more doubt-filled time.

Remember the list from Winter about common ways we slide into the darker, stormier mindsets?

1. Fear of rejection (they won't want me)
2. Fear of judgment (what'll they think?)
3. Fear of failure (I just can't do it)
4. Fear of success (who am I to succeed?)
5. Fear of surpassing your parent's success
6. Trying to satisfy everyone (people pleaser)
7. Indecisiveness (I'll make the wrong choice)
8. Stuck in complain-mode (always half-empty)
9. Jumping to blame someone/something else.
10. Comparison-it is (everyone else is better)
11. Perfectionism (you must be perfect)
12. Burn-out (can't stop, won't stop)
13. Hoarding control (it's about trust)
14. Mom-guilt/dad-guilt (oh the guilt!)
15. Superwoman Syndrome (only 'I' can save the day)
16. Firestarter Fixation (we start fires to stay busy)
17. Shiny Object Syndrome (jumping from new thing to new thing searching for *theee thing*.)
18. Having zero fun for a really long time.

Which one of these consistently pushes you into Fall? That's your self-sabotage tactic. It's where your pattern lies. It's your gateway to the darkness. That's what you need to build an antidote for.

Without question, these are all slippery slopes, but with the meteoric rise in social media marketing, one is escalating to be a super destructive force for entrepreneurs and I want to talk about it separately. Let's see how Comparisonitis creates massive disconnection from our business brilliance.

Comparisonitis

We all know the feeling: Janie launches her book to bestseller status. Priyanka has a full calendar of clients from her first month. Heather posts online that she made $20,000 in the first three months of her business. Zara announces she hit 100,000 downloads on her podcast. Nica sells her training event out every month. Maria-Elena wins a huge contract that means more money, more visibility, and more impact.

Meanwhile we're sitting here, adding up our expenses, wondering what they have that we don't have. They must be smarter. Know more power players. Have it all figured out. They are meant for this.

Oh, hello Fall. There you are.

> *"Comparison is the thief of joy."*
> ~ *Theodore Roosevelt*

We are not them. We are us.

We need to stay in our own lane. We need to focus on our journey. We don't know where their route started or even where they're going, and we don't know how they are defining success.

Let's think about lanes and cars. You have a car, and the person you're comparing yourself to also has a car. Their car is sooo nice and fancy. But wait!

- We don't know if their car came with extra features from the factory (Do they bring a specialized degree or deep corporate experience?)
- We don't know if they did some after-market upgrades (Did they recently complete a certificate program or post-graduate training?)
- We don't know if they had some parts removed to make way for the ONE thing they will focus on and be amazing at? (Does their business serve a niche audience and nothing else?)
- We don't know if they're driving alone or with a group (Do they have a spouse/partner/ friend providing specialty services to help them out?)
- We don't know if they bought the extended warranty program so if they have any issues, professional problem-solvers are ready to help. (Especially in Winter-prone finance, legal, tech)

What do we really know? We know about us.

We've got to stay in our lane and remember what it took us to get through our Spring Cleaning and arrive in Summer. We need to go back to those practices and focus on ourselves.

"The only one you should compare yourself to is you. Your mission is to become better today than you were yesterday."

~ John Maxwell, Author and Pastor

When We Are Ready to Leave Fall

Leaving Fall and heading back to the beautiful, connected days of Summer means we need to remember that dreaming isn't doing.

When fall comes in real life, the leaves change color and the temperature drops. In *The 5 Seasons of Connection*, Fall is less tactile. We insult ourselves, or put ourselves down, but there are no visible, outward signs so we think it's just the way things happen.

Fall can (and does!) happen at any time but we need to catch it early, identify what caused it to arrive this time, decide on what habits will prevent it next time, and bring yourself back to Summer. That's where you feel connected to your business brilliance and all that entails: your confidence, your positive contributions to your client's lives, and your income.

What happens when you're struggling in Fall, wanting to go back to Summer, but anxious that you're headed toward Winter?

You have arrived at the Crossroads, our 5th season.

CHAPTER 6

Crossroads

THIS IS THE SEASON WE HAVE BEEN WAITING FOR!

O ur journey started with the cold, disconnected season of Winter. We felt burdened and buried by our negative thoughts and beliefs.

We moved to the next season where Spring Cleaning cleared away a lot of damage and debris. We explored new ways to connect to our best self.

After planting the seeds in Spring, we fully enjoyed Summer, the sweetest season full of growth, beauty, joy, fullness, warmth, and the fruits of our labor. Here, our confidence and our businesses thrive while we deepen connections to key people, explore new ideas, and honor the practices we put in place to keep us fulfilled, rested, and ready for any weather.

In Fall, we noticed we weren't paying attention to our garden and it suffered from neglect. Weeds popped up and critters creeped in, threatening our harvest. When we think everything is going great, we stop noticing the small signs, the little inconsistencies in our thoughts or behaviors. We don't see that our connection is slipping, and we enter Fall.

We can get back to Summer with dedication and intentional work, but it won't happen because you wish it to, want it to, or force it to.

The 5th season is where you hold the ultimate influence over your outcome. It's where the power lies. It's choice. It's possibility.

It's the Crossroads.

> *"Between stimulus and response, there is a space. In that space is our power to choose our response. In our response lies our growth and our freedom."*
>
> ~ **Viktor E. Frankl,**
> **Neurologist and Psychologist**

What is the Crossroads?

When we are at the Crossroads, we may feel:

- Torn between reacting (moves us to Winter) and responding (moves us to Summer).
- Anxious about which path to take.
- Worried about what decision to make.
- Emotional, withdrawn, and hesitant all at once.
- Eager to get through an issue at any cost.
- Intent on gathering all info before choosing, sometimes sitting in analysis paralysis.

The 5th season is the most visited season of all. You could face the Crossroads ten, twenty, thirty times a day. You could swing from Summer to Fall to Summer to Fall to Winter to Spring to Summer in an afternoon. Between every shift you'll come to the Crossroads. In other words, every single time you have thoughts, feelings, internal or external conversations, think something or do something in or about your business, you will be at the Crossroads.

Every interaction is a choice.

If we hear of someone's amazing success, do we genuinely congratulate them? Or do we smile while belittling ourselves over why that isn't our success story? When someone returns our product for their money back, do we get curious about why it didn't work or do we use it as evidence we aren't any good?

The Crossroads is the moment we pause, first to reflect, then to respond, reducing the force and intensity of our reactions.

> *"It is our choices, Harry, that show what we truly are, far more than our abilities."*
>
> ***~Albus Dumbledore,***
> ***Headmaster of Hogwarts***

The Pause

Why is there so much power in the pause?

First and foremost, it gives us time to assess where we are in the moment. Are we coming from a place of fullness or depletion? What hot button was pushed? Was a trigger activated?

Second, the pause gives us the opportunity to choose how we'll handle the situation. Maybe it's an opportunity to step away so we can reflect on all the components before making a judgment or decision.

Maybe it's a chance to lean in, asking questions to learn more about the issue before moving forward.

Or maybe it's an opportunity to sit silently and hold space for your thoughts until you find your center. In this scenario, ANTs may knock at your door and bark something negative to jolt you into action, but your heart will whisper at the same time. Your heart will tell you what you know is true.

Holding space allows both to show up, then you decide which way you'll go. Let's explore this more.

Holding Space

Holding space often refers to our ability to sit quietly, calmly, and without imparting wisdom or influence. When we hold space for ourselves, it means we're willing to be on our journey without judgment, criticism, or without needing to jump in to fix it.

We recognize that it just *is*.

Holding space is sitting patiently at the Crossroads without being invested in a specific outcome, even if you have ideas or solutions that you're sure will make it all go away quickly. Sometimes speed is your partner, but at the Crossroads, speed could keep you spinning when you haven't fully processed the issue.

When we hold space, allow anything and everything to arise. We exist in the now. (Integrating your Internal Spring Cleaning strategy of journaling here is particularly helpful.)

Opposing Feelings

The internal conflict you feel at the Crossroads is a true struggle because it sets up two opposing feelings.

On the one hand, you may be very angry, hurt, disappointed, or frustrated with yourself or your situation. Someone or something poked your fear or pushed your hot button. You might fall into the world of 'un-': unworthy, unreliable, undeserving, unable, unfocused, unsure, unbelievably upset.

On the other hand, you may feel ready to solve it, resolve it, control it, or contain it. You might want to make it better or make it go away. You may feel sad, but you know you can handle it. You look inside, explore your vast collection of internal and external resources, and know you have overcome other obstacles before. Here there is no panic, no reactivity.

Both feelings are valid and real.

If you berate, shame, ridicule, criticize, mock, judge, or insult yourself or someone in your business, you will absolutely find yourself in Winter.

If you inquire, validate, empathize, or simply think or listen, you'll most likely end up in Spring, maybe even Summer. This doesn't mean that you won't feel angry, hurt, or disappointed; it just means that you're choosing not to act out your feelings in a negative way.

The First of Many

You will face many situations for the first time on your entrepreneurial journey: the first time you lose a sale. The first time you stop yourself because you're afraid. The first time you speak up and then feel flooded with shame that you've said the wrong thing. The first time you overpromised or underdelivered. The first time you let your client or yourself down.

As an entrepreneur, there'll be no shortage of opportunities for you to stand at the Crossroads.

Even if you haven't had direct experience with a first time issue *exactly*, you've likely faced other situations where you stood at the Crossroads and had to choose between two options. Leverage those past experiences to assist with future events. Despite the release of adrenalin, the flooding of fight or flight responses, or a barrage of negative thoughts, you can use calming techniques. Practice deep breathing and respond as if you were talking to a respected elder instead of your out-of-control mindset.

This is not to say that you should deny your feelings and suppress your reaction. We're humans living a human experience. However, there's a difference between how you *feel* and how you *express*.

At the Crossroads, you'll need to build a bridge of connectiveness between where you are and where you want to be to stay in Summer. Focus on feelings that come from a place of grace, forgiveness, learning, doing your best, and teaching.

Indra was an incredible cross-stitch artist. She wanted to share her love by teaching others the craft, create products to sell, and add to her family income.

She purchased a course to learn how to launch a membership site for her audience. She spent weeks setting up the site, creating content, and building anticipation with her followers.

On launch day, she sent an invitation for people to join, and sat back waiting for the members to roll in.

Crickets.

She refreshed her page a dozen times. Her heart raced. No one. Why wasn't anyone joining? She worked hard for weeks, what happened?

"A year ago I would've burst into tears and turned everything off, convinced I was making a fool of myself and my family," Indra told me. "I would've closed my curtains, turned off my phone, and hid from the world. I wouldn't want anyone's pity so I would've carried on as if it never happened.

"But, then I learned about the seasons, and discovered that my go-to Fall and Winter responses stem from shame. When my launch failed, my instinct was to panic and hide, but for the first time in my life I didn't. I got curious. Why didn't anyone sign up? Let me go through the process.

"Well, wouldn't you know that I had listed the launch date wrong, I was a week early! I then launched the next week and twenty-nine members signed up. Can you imagine if I did what I always did and just shut it all down? I would've missed out on everything because I was leading from fear. My time at the Crossroads changed my life!"

~ Indra, artist
and membership site master

The Crossroads is there when you're faced with a decision in the moment, but it also allows you to evaluate your current path and decide if it still fits your business.

There have been times when entrepreneurs were headed down one path and noticed that pressure and stress had started to build. They created a Crossroads right there to check in and see if they were aligned or if they needed to course correct.

Course Corrections

Lisa was gaining momentum in her business and she was exceeding her targets. She should have been thrilled, but she felt stressed, pulled, and agitated.

"I thought I was building the business of my dreams," she said, "but I didn't go through the exercise of defining success. No matter how hard I worked, something just wasn't fitting me perfectly. I was moody and unhappy. I didn't know what it was, and frankly I was too busy to even think about it.

"One day my mom experienced a medical emergency and I rescheduled everything in my business to be at her bedside. I was antsy at first, but then took this as a time to pause, reflect, and refocus.

"I was at a Crossroads. I knew if I kept going on my current path, I'd end up in Winter, no doubt. But in the quiet hospital room, in the freedom of a totally unscheduled day to do nothing, I heard a quiet voice inside that I had never heard before. My time at the Crossroads completely shifted my energy, focus, my business and my level of happiness. Stepping back and course correcting was exactly what I needed."

~ Lisa, nutritionist
and gut-health expert

You've Been at the Crossroads Before

Think back to another time in your life when you felt angry, hurt, or disappointed. How did you come through that experience? Did you:

- Journal?
- Talk to a colleague or loved one?
- Recommit to a desired outcome and move on?

Even though being at the Crossroads may feel uncomfortable or stressful, we're blessed to have a lifetime of experiences to use as a resource. On top of using our past experiences to guide us along our business journey, we can also use our time at the Crossroads to tap into our 6th sense. Our intuition.

Intuition

Intuition is the ability to understand something without any evidence or conscious reasoning. It can play a critical role in our lives if we allow it.

We may feel our intuition kick into overdrive many times on the entrepreneurial journey, like when we have a hunch about a client, or when we hesitate to sign a contract, somehow we just know there is more!

Being still and listening to that inner voice can guide you through a particularly tough Crossroads.

> *"The intuitive mind is a sacred gift and the rational mind is a faithful servant. We have created a society that honors the servant and has forgotten the gift."*
>
> *~ Albert Einstein,*
> *Theoretical Physicist, Author*

Felicia's business was booming. She had too much work and not enough time. Someone recommended she sub-contract parts of the projects out to other freelancers to get through the crunch. She didn't like the idea because her clients appreciated her high-touch relationships, but she just couldn't keep up.

One man came highly recommended but in their first conversation, Felicia had the feeling that he wasn't being honest about his projects and abilities and talked down to her. Nonetheless, Felicia hired him.

Instead of trusting her intuition and ending the relationship, she gave him very important work to allow him to show off his skills and abilities.

After a few mishaps, Felicia's client nearly fired her because of his substandard work. She sacrificed her business brilliance because she didn't trust her intuition and rushed into hiring the wrong person.

> *"Stop telling yourself you don't know what to do. Yes, you do. Listen to your intuition and trust yourself."*
>
> *~ Katherine Sullivan,*
> *Founder of Marketing Solved*

As entrepreneurs, I believe we're deeply connected to our work. We know when things are shifting, often before the physical evidence appears.

But our logical, rational side often overpowers our 6th sense. We second-guess ourselves, or even worse, mock ourselves for having an active imagination. Our intuition isn't a magic power that will lead us astray. It's actually our brain's true superpower.

Our brain collects, categorizes, and synthesizes thousands of pieces of information around us, whether we're conscious of it or not. It then takes this data and forms a worldview feeding our intuition.

To tap into the deeper reserves of our brain's capabilities and make well-informed, well-supported decisions while at the Crossroads, we need to quiet our inner and outer noise. We need to explore all our thoughts and feelings without filtering them through our mind's logical, rational, evidence-based filter.

When we stand at the Crossroads, we can build a bridge or burn it, but only one of them brings you to deeper connection with your business brilliance.

This 5th and final season is the last one we need to master so we can guide our business and growth more smoothly. We can skillfully read the weather forecasts and know if pressure is building and a storm is coming, or if glorious, sunny skies are ahead. And sometimes we might be blessed with art in the sky.

Watch for Rainbows

A rainbow is an arc of color that appears when millions of water droplets reflect sunlight in the sky.

Historically and symbolically, rainbows have held a mystical role in our culture. The fact that these awe-inspiring gifts from nature often follow the harshest, darkest storms has led us to believe that rainbows are the promise of hope and the presence of blessings. We can't touch them, feel them, or save them for later, but when they light up the sky, we appreciate their beauty.

On our business journey, a rainbow could appear unexpectedly in the middle of an interaction. It's something we might miss if our heads were down or we were spotlighting on a small portion of the scene.

When we're pausing at the Crossroads, we can listen, think, and notice these gifts. Sometimes the rainbow is the bridge from one season to another.

What does a rainbow on your journey look like?

Maybe someone who didn't buy your offering comes back a few weeks later and buys one for herself and one for her friend, helping you meet your revenue goals. Perhaps something you really needed for your business was included in a flash sale, saving you a lot of money. Maybe someone posted a glowing review of your business online, and you found it by accident!

These rainbow moments are fleeting and easy to miss so I encourage you to actively look for them.

Now that we understand the powers of all the seasons—and how to navigate each one—let's explore how deeply they impact our lives. In Part 2, we get BUSY! The next five chapters will help us dig into all the nooks and crannies of our values, strengths, skills, abilities, areas of growth, and our hopes and goals.

"When you have once seen the glow of happiness on the face of a beloved person, you know that a man can have no vocation but to awaken that light on the faces surrounding him. In the depth of winter, I finally learned that within me there lay an invincible summer."

~ Albert Camus, Philosopher and Author

PART 2

CHAPTER 7

The Five Elements of Awareness

F*ive specific elements help* entrepreneurs master their mindset, providing us with:

- Greater understanding of ourselves.
- Deeper connection to our business goals
- More compassion for our areas of growth.
- Collaborative problem-solving efforts.
- Stronger systems that support us at every step.

These benefit you during the ups and downs—or Summers and Winters—of your business. From your first day of business until your last, there will be ample opportunity for growth and self-discovery, supported by the foundation of the Five Elements of Awareness.

Implementing these in our business allows us to grow in each season and uncover more layers of our business brilliance. Let's be honest—just because we know how to avoid Winter doesn't mean we always will; we'll slip into Winter again. We'll feel dark, go dark, and be dark. Our inner critic will rage all over us, stomping on every little sprout that we carefully and lovingly planted in our last Spring cycle.

It's vital we know our seasons, but it's equally critical that we know who we are and what we bring to our business so our brilliance can easily shine.

How do we do this?

We get really intimate with our business. We study it, looking at it from many angles. We experience it. We examine all the parts so when the storms come—and they will—we'll bend, but not break.

The Five Elements of Awareness are:

1. KAST Inventory
2. Personal Core Values
3. Purpose, Company Values, Mission, Vision
4. SWOT
5. Goals and Priorities

The more you know about these five foundational elements, the smoother your road to becoming the confident and capable entrepreneur you want to be.

Sometimes to avoid Winter, we need intervention. In these times, we rely on our own Five Elements of Awareness, a practical and personalized toolbox with all the right equipment to guide us back to Summer.

CHAPTER 8

Element One: KAST Inventory

I *picked up a popular* entrepreneurial magazine recently. The main headline was, "If you aren't reaching the moon, you aren't stretching far enough."

Now, on a good day, I might think:

> "Yes, I must stretch a little further."
> "I *could* call a few more prospects."
> "I'm ready to sign a few more clients."
> "I'll sell a few more products."

But, not all days are good days. As an entrepreneur, some days feel like you're one step away from throwing it all in and joining a drumming circle! On days like these, we don't need to hear all the ways we aren't making millions every month, like some claim we should.

Today, we're going deep inside. Grab a flashlight, a pencil, a notebook, and a snack.

Come in with me.

First we'll examine our KAST. Not broken-arm cast, not a Broadway cast, but KAST, which stands for:

K nowledge
A bility
S kills
T alents and Natural Gifts

Whether you've been in business for ten minutes or ten years, you've many resources at your fingertips.

(K) Knowledge	Everything you have ever learned, from every different source.
(A) Ability	What you can do without effort.
(S) Skills	What you have learned through practice, education, training, and trial-and-error.
(T) Talents & Natural Gifts	Your unique, special gifts such as artistic talents, incredible physical strength, musical genius, charisma, or powerful personal energy.

Many entrepreneurs in their Winter storms feel inadequate or unworthy because they can't find their value or see their business brilliance.

We will change that right now.

I've modified a KAS inventory list for us to use, originally published by the UC Davis Career Center.

From this list, select everything *in* you right now.

The things you have learned.

The things you always knew.

The things you can do.

The things you understand.

The things you can teach.

The things you experienced.

Go on, amaze yourself with everything you have *inside you today* that make up your business brilliance.

Verbal Communication

___ Speak/articulate clearly in group settings

___ Express opinions without offending

___ Interview people to obtain information

___ Handle complaints respectfully

___ Present ideas effectively and logically

___ Influence others to see a new point of view

___ Sell ideas, products, or services

___ Debate ideas with others

___ Participate in group discussions and teams

___ Negotiate terms of agreements and contracts

___ Provide constructive feedback

___ Provide sufficient info when you delegate

Nonverbal Communication

___ Listen carefully and attentively

___ Convey a positive self-image

___ Use body language to make others at ease

___ Develop rapport easily with groups

___ Establish culture to support learning

___ Express feelings through body language

___ Believe in self worth

___ Respond to non-verbal cues

___ Model behavior or concepts for others

___ Accept feedback by listening thoroughly

___ Speak in sign language or other non-verbal ways

Written Communication

____ Capture ideas from brainstorming

____ Construct reports and operating documents

____ Write poetry, fiction, plays, or stories

____ Write proposals for service

____ Create invoices or terms of agreement

____ Write sales and advertising copy

____ Edit and proofread written material

____ Utilize all forms of technology for writing

____ Write clearly, concisely, and in logical order

____ Create to-do lists and prioritize items

____ Demonstrate expertise in grammar/style

____ Express emotion using words or pictures

Train/Consult

____ Teach, advise, coach, empower

____ Conduct assessments of what is needed

____ Use a variety of media for presentation

____ Develop educational/training materials

____ Create and deliver a plan for something

____ Facilitate a group

____ Explain difficult ideas or complex topics

____ Assess learning styles and respond

____ Consult and recommend solutions

____ Encourage sharing ideas/strategies

____ Reach visual/auditory/kinesthetic learners

Leadership

____ Being calm under pressure

____ Know what you stand for and share it

____ Envision the future and lead change

____ Establish policy, rules, regulations, and systems

____ Set goals and determine courses of action

____ Motivate/inspire others to achieve goals

____ Create solutions to complex problems

____ Develop and mentor talent

____ Take risks, make hard decisions, and be decisive

____ Encourage the use of technology at all levels

____ Delegate tasks to appropriate people

____ Eliminate projects or programs as needed

____ Terminate relationships when necessary

____ Ask relevant and forward-moving questions

Analyze

____ Study data or behavior for ideas/solutions

____ Analyze patterns, numbers, trends

____ Identify areas needing more information

____ Compare and evaluate information

____ Systematize information and results

____ Apply curiosity

____ Investigate clues

____ Use technology for analysis

____ See what is missing from data/research

Research

_____ Identify appropriate information sources

_____ Search written, oral, and technological info

_____ Interview primary sources

_____ Hypothesize and test for results

_____ Compile numerical and statistical data

_____ Classify and sort information into categories

_____ Gather info from a number of sources

_____ Patiently search for hard-to-find info

_____ Utilize electronic search methods

_____ Read industry magazines, articles, books

_____ Listen to interviews/podcasts in your field

_____ Attend seminars, trainings, and conferences

_____ Follow industry leaders on social media

Plan and Organize

_____ Identify and organize tasks or information

_____ Coordinate people, activities, and details

_____ Develop a plan and set objectives

_____ Set up and keep time schedules

_____ Anticipate problems and identify solutions

_____ Develop realistic goals/actions in response

_____ Arrange correct sequence of info/actions

_____ Create guidelines for implementing action

_____ Create efficient systems

_____ Follow through and insure completion of a task

_____ Plan and oversee events, meetings, parties

_____ Manage all components required for events

Counsel and Serve

____ Counsel, advise, consult, and guide others

____ Care for and serve people in need

____ Provide empathy, sensitivity, and patience

____ Collect info or resources to help others

____ Help people make their own decisions

____ Help others improve health and welfare

____ Listen with empathy and objectivity

____ Coach, guide, and encourage others

____ Mediate peace between conflicting parties

____ Knowledge of self-help theories/programs

____ Facilitate self-awareness in others

Interpersonal Relations

____ Convey a sense of humor

____ Anticipate needs and reactions

____ Express feelings appropriately

____ Understand others and their behavior

____ Encourage, empower, and advocate for people

____ Create positive, hospitable environments

____ Adjust plans for the unexpected

____ Facilitate conflict management

____ Communicate well with diverse groups

____ Hear message when receiving feedback

____ Maintain discretion

Create and Innovate

____ Visualize concepts and results

____ Imagine in color, shape, and form

____ Brainstorm and make use of group synergy

____ Communicate with metaphors

____ Invent products through experimentation

____ Express ideas through art

____ Remember faces, accurate spatial memory

____ Create images through design and sketch

____ Sculpt, carve, form, mold, paint, sew, draw

____ Utilize computer software for creation

____ Be imaginative

____ Curate and share art and artistic examples

Management

____ Manage personnel, projects, and time

____ Foster a sense of ownership in employees

____ Delegate tasks and review performance

____ Increase efficiency to achieve goals

____ Develop and facilitate work teams

____ Provide training for development of staff

____ Adjust plans/procedures for the unexpected

____ Facilitate conflict management

____ Utilize technology to facilitate management

____ Meet deadlines

____ Hire the right people to support growth

____ Recruit others or reallocate resources

Financial

____ Calculate or perform math computations

____ Work with precision with numerical data

____ Keep accurate, complete financial records

____ Perform accounting functions

____ Compile data and apply statistical analysis

____ Create graphs and charts for presentation

____ Use computer software for records/analysis

____ Forecast, estimate expenses and income

____ Appraise and analyze costs

____ Create and justify organization's budget

____ Complete tax requirements

____ Pay bills on time

Administrative

____ Receive and manage paperwork

____ Identify and purchase necessary materials

____ Utilize computer software and equipment

____ Organize, improve, and adapt systems

____ Track progress of projects and troubleshoot

____ Achieve goals within budget/time schedule

____ Assign tasks, set standards for support staff

____ Hire and supervise temporary personnel

____ Demonstrate flexibility during crisis

____ Oversee communication via email and phone

____ Order necessary products and services

Technology

____ Send, receive, forward, and archive email

____ Navigate social media (Facebook, LinkedIn)

____ Set up online banking or investing accounts

____ Register for online money system (PayPal)

____ Print electronic documents if you need them

____ Write documents (Word/Google Docs)

____ Create spreadsheets (Excel/Google Sheets)

____ Create slides for presentation (PowerPoint)

____ Set up invoice system to receive payments

____ Book appointments online (calendar app)

____ Upload, sort, catalog, and use photos/videos

____ Update website content: words and images

Construct and Operate

____ Assemble and install equipment

____ Build a structure, follow proper sequence

____ Repair broken machines or equipment

____ Use tools and machines

Are there others you want to include?

Whew! That was huge! When I first skimmed the list, I discounted many items because I hadn't done them at a job. Technically true.

I may not have mastered all these at a job, but I did master them elsewhere: as a mom of three busy kids, volunteering at schools, being a PTA president, serving as an HOA treasurer, or booking intricate trips for my family to travel around the world.

*Where you acquired the skills isn't
important. Having them is the key.*

Take a look at your list. Are there things you excel at that surprise you? Are you astonished by how many of these you can do right now, without another day of training, another dollar for courses, or another expert teaching you his ways?

You are resource-rich, my friend!

All the traits you checked off, plus others that may not be on the list, are the resources you can count on to run your business. They work hand in hand with our unseen thoughts to make decisions. Wait, if we aren't aware of these thoughts, where do they come from?

It's time to identify our Core Values.

CHAPTER 9

Element Two: Core Values

The greatest advice for entrepreneurs seeking their business brilliance came a thousand years ago:

"Know thyself."
— *written on the temple of the oracle in Delphi*

How do you *know thyself?* Enter Core Values.

Whether you're aware of it or not, your Core Values are the pulse and power beneath your decisions. They're the rules that guide you through life's ups and downs. They determine your answers to questions like *who am I?* and *what do I stand for?* Core Values help you set priorities. They are the fundamental forces that drive your decisions.

Let's test it.

Decide if you agree/disagree with the following:

- It's fine to fudge on the bookkeeping—a few bucks here or there doesn't matter.
- Selling products at the cheapest price is best.
- If I'm not grinding, I'm not going to succeed.
- I'll get big loans now and it'll pay off someday.
- The key to success is to take huge risks.
- If I want it done right, I must do it myself.

Whether you agree or disagree with these statements is based solely on your Core Values.

Look at the list again.

Do you know someone who would answer differently? You very well might! Whether it's someone else in your family, at work, or in your community, you likely know someone who is similar to you in many ways but then *boom*—you fall into an argument over strategy, ethics, or economics and you just can't believe she thinks that way.

Chances are, you were having a values conflict. Different things matter to each of you.

When you start listening to conversations around you, it becomes easier to identify people's deeply-rooted belief systems.

> *"Your values create your internal compass that can navigate how you make decisions in your life. If you compromise your core values, you go nowhere."*
>
> *~ Roy T. Bennett, Author*

Recently, I was at an event and I heard two women discussing a situation one of them was facing.

Woman 1: She knows the deal. She signed the contract. She knew there were no refunds, no matter what. Now, she's coming for a refund? I paid my designer, bought everything we needed. It's too bad she can't attend the class but she signed the contract.

Woman 2: She just lost her job and she's alone with two kids. She's probably terrified she can't pay rent.

Woman 1: If she completes my class, she can make back her investment, plus more. She signed a contract.

Woman 2: But, when she signed the contract, she didn't know she'd be jobless. Doesn't that change it?

Woman 1: Would it change things for the bank if she took out a loan? Or a dealership if she financed a car?

Who are you siding with here? Both women are successful in their own businesses, but they make very different decisions and hold different ideals based on their core values. Where you stand is a testimony to your values. Why is that important to uncover your business brilliance?

Knowing your Core Values gives you a clear and solid framework to make better decisions for your business, your team, and your clients.

Our Core Values are the beliefs that form our worldview and philosophical perspective. They define us. They are the basis for the values we fight for on a big scale like justice or equality, as well as on a small scale like how we run our lives and our businesses.

They help guide our choices in tough situations. They become our automatic responses when we're challenged or pushed. Our Core Values also influence what we believe *and* what we're willing to believe every day as entrepreneurs.

Your values have been passed down through generations. They combine the experience of your life, your parent's lives, and their parents before them. Some of these are rooted in culture or religion, some are based in privilege, hardships, or survival.

> *"The more attention we can devote to helping developing leaders tune in to their core values –drawing on their real experience and their true aspirations in life - the more likely it is they'll make smart choices about how and where to invest their talents."*
>
> ~ *Stewart D. Friedman,*
> *Professor and Author*

Knowing your Core Values will benefit your business decisions right away, so let's dive in.

Exercise: Identifying Your Core Values

Answer each question without too much thought.

What's important to me? What matters deeply?

_____

_____

What character traits are the most important to me?

_____

_____

What words describe my deepest beliefs?

_____

_____

What are the principles I fight for in an argument?

_____

_____

What organizations do I support/champion?

_____

_____

How does your list look? Does it reflect you?

It's okay if you have five words or fifteen words at this stage. We'll add a few more, then whittle the list down. Some people find it difficult to think of the right words without prompts, so below is a list of top Core Values to get you started. Select the words that speak to you, that feel important, and define you.

Alternatively, when you see a word that provokes anger or frustration, think about its opposite as a potential Core Value. (Also make a note so you can dig deeper into why it holds so much power over you.)

Don't select a word because you think it looks or sounds better than another word—there are no points given out for a list that *looks* amazing.

Many women admit in their first shot at selecting words, they picked traits they knew their partners, parents, or friends would like, not words that were truly self-reflective. Be as true to *you* as you can be.

Also, be mindful that who you are and who you want to be are at the heart of this exercise. Not who you have been or who you think you should be.

Go through the following list and select what words bring you fulfillment, joy, bliss, meaning, and purpose. If there are words that pop into mind that are not here, please add them because this is your list!

Also, words have dictionary meanings, but they also have cultural and geographical significance. Feel free to select words that mean what they mean to you.

Without overthinking, select 5-10 words.

Core Value List

Write your selected words here, including the words you may have come up with on your own.

_____	_____	_____
_____	_____	_____
_____	_____	_____

Now look at your list. For each one, think about how it makes you feel. What comes to your mind when you see that word? Are there themes? Maybe you selected a few words that mean the same thing? Make a note of that.

Core Value List

Acceptance	Encouraging	Loyalty
Accessibility	Energetic	Meticulous
Accomplish	Entrepreneur	Mindful
Accurate	Environment	Nature
Achieve	Ethical	Openness
Adventure	Excellence	Optimism
Ambition	Fair	Organized
Appreciation	Faith	Patient
Assertiveness	Family	Patriotic
Authentic	Fearless	Persistent
Authority	Flexible	Philanthropy
Balance	Freedom	Play
Beauty	Friendships	Pleasure
Bold	Fun	Positive
Brave	Generosity	Practical
Calm	Gratitude	Prepared
Capable	Happiness	Private
Caring	Hard working	Productive
Challenge	Health	Realistic
Charitable	Helpful	Reliable
Cleanliness	Honesty	Resilient
Collaborative	Humor	Resourceful
Community	Impact	Results-focus
Compassion	Impartial	Reputation
Competent	Independent	Respect
Competitive	Innovative	Responsible
Connected	Inquisitive	Self-Aware
Cooperation	Inspiring	Self-Respect
Courageous	Integrity	Service
Creative	Intelligent	Spirituality
Curious	Intuitive	Simplicity
Daring	Justice	Stability
Decisive	Kindness	Success
Dependable	Knowledge	Thoughtful
Determined	Lawful	Traditional
Diligent	Leadership	Trustworthy
Disciplined	Learning	Truth
Education	Listening	Unique
Efficient	Logical	Wealth
Empathetic	Love	Wisdom

When you've reflected on each word, go back through the list and circle your top ten. Choose the words that really resonate with you, made you smile, or gave a sense of comfort, joy or purpose. Add your words here.

_____	_____
_____	_____
_____	_____
_____	_____
_____	_____

Reread your list and make sure they feel good.

Now, pick the top five that absolutely define you. Words that if someone heard the list, they would know it described you. I know it's hard to pick your top favorites from a *list* of favorites, but you can do it!

To help confirm your list is an accurate reflection of your true Core Values, consider these questions:

- How deeply does this define me or my choices?
- How hard would I fight for this value?
- Do I consider this essential to me?
- Does this represent how I truly am in the world?

Chances are high that at this point, you can remove another word or two from this list.

If you're feeling hesitant or resistant, go back to the initial super list. See if you'd like to swap out any of your top choices for one that might have slipped through the cracks the first time. Oftentimes, this can help you see your list with a fresh perspective. You may have an easier time removing 2-3 that are amazing, but not *core* values.

Write down your top words.

_____ _____ _____

_____ _____

Congratulations on doing this critical exercise!

When we have a clearly defined set of Core Values, we avoid making decisions that go against who we want to be. It gives us the courage to say yes when we mean yes, and no when we mean no.

As an important step in laying the foundation for the Five Elements of Awareness, knowing your Core Values will guide your rules, routines, structures, and systems as you travel along your business journey.

If you skipped that exercise, don't worry. You'll still be using your Core Values to drive your business, you just won't be actively aware of which direction you'll go. Knowing who you are and what you stand for helps you prioritize the right things for you.

Two Partners, Two Core Value Systems

(This section is for entrepreneurs who have others in decision-making positions in their businesses. If you're a solopreneur, please move on to the next chapter.)

For some business owners, there isn't one single value system at play. Each partner brings their own history, experiences, and beliefs to the table. If your business has more than one person at the helm (whether you co-own your business with another family member, parent, or a trusted friend, you have loyal employees in senior positions in your business, or your life partner is deeply invested in your professional success) then frequent or repeated misunderstandings, conflict, or arguments between the key players can happen when two systems clash.

In two-partner businesses, it's best if both parties complete their own value list. Your operations, speed/scale of growth, risk management, and hiring decisions are influenced by two separate and independent sets of Core Values. We often don't know if we're aligned or misaligned until something pushes a hot button and elicits two very different reactions.

Let's see how this unfolded for one business.

Nora and Tessa met at a craft fair and discovered they both loved the look and feel of handmade soaps. The two became friends. A few months later, they became business partners to make soaps and scrubs with natural ingredients. They both valued quality ingredients, loved the planet, and wanted to create a product they could be proud to share.

They invested their savings into materials, equipment, molds, and the business licensing and registrations for their city. They were so excited!

Nora took pride in blending petals, herbs, and oils in the soap, hand mixing the elements and cutting them into intricate shapes. She was a true artist.

Tessa preferred to create simple soaps to get them done, out, and sold without intensive labor.

Tessa pressed Nora to focus on making affordable and pretty-but-plain soaps at first, adding fancy shapes and scents later. Nora pushed Tessa to find buyers who would pay $20 per bar of specialty soap to cover the cost of materials, ingredients, and her labor.

Their bubbly relationship hit hard times. After a few blowouts, their soap dreams went down the drain.

What happened here?

Nora valued creative expression and high-artistry, using premium ingredients to make products women would admire, cherish, and enjoy as a reward. Tessa valued affordability and accessibility, selling good products that any woman could enjoy any day.

They'd aligned on some of their values, but they didn't have the Core Value discussion which goes deeper than 'I'm-so-excited-we-are-doing-this.' Doing it would've avoided their unfortunate crash and burn.

Combining Core Values

Take two sheets of paper, and on the first write *Combined Values*. Take the second sheet and fold it in half. List your Core Values on one half of the sheet and your partner's Core Values on the other half.

Are there overlapping beliefs or duplications? If you both value philanthropy, cross it out on each of your lists and write it on the first sheet you titled *Combined Values*. Now let's explore what's left.

I recommend both partners share their list in a relaxed manner because open-mindedness is vital here. For each word, take time to explain the history, the meaning, and why it's so profound.

Now, change roles.

The speaker is now the listener, and the second partner will share their Core Value list.

After both partners are done, work together to select 5-6 combined core values for your partnership.

This exercise accomplishes a few things.

First, it gives both partners time and space to share experiences that shaped them from a young age and continue to guide their decisions, preferences, and actions. Being open, honest, and vulnerable allows the bond between you to deepen significantly.

Second, it allows you to see where there is alignment, or shared values, as well as where there is misalignment, or potential for hurt, disappointment, anger, or frustration. Partners have reported that completing this exercise greatly improved their friendship and their business relationship.

Third, it blends values that you both hold dear to create a business legacy, which may endure for many years and touch countless lives.

> *"It's not hard to make decisions when you know what your values are."*
>
> **~ Roy E. Disney, nephew of Walt Disney**

CHAPTER 10

Element Three: Purpose, Values, Vision, Mission

N ow that we've explored our Core Values, it's time to stretch a little further and create a few guiding principles to define our company's purpose, values, mission, and vision.

These may sound the same, or even a bit interchangeable, but we can break them down and see how they are all pieces of a more complete picture.

Purpose	Our big why. Why are we creating our business? Why do we work so hard at it?
Values	These guide everything we do and inform all decisions in our business, from A-Z.
Vision	Where we're headed, painting the picture of our future so we know our destination.
Mission	This is how we plan to achieve our vision today, tomorrow, and the next day.

Why does this information matter when you just lost a huge sale, or didn't make your monthly target, or made a costly tech error hurting your quarter?

When we don't know why we're working so hard, what we stand for, what our dream business looks like, or how to get there, we're more vulnerable to Winter. We're also prone to staying there longer. I don't want that for you. You don't want that for you!

When you know your Purpose, Values, Vision and Mission, you'll know why you're investing your time, energy, resources, heart, and soul into your business, even when it's hard. Especially when it's hard.

It might feel like a LOT to do four different exercises, and I don't want you to be overwhelmed. Read through this chapter, make some notes, and come back to it when you have some time to dedicate to your key ideas. These four different components are interconnected and really are four leaves on the same branch—definitely not four different trees!

Purpose

When we think of purpose, think about the big reason why we're running our business.

Why did you start it? What promise did you make to your clients about why you're in business? What do you want to achieve in running your business?

Your purpose statement is a short sentence about why you exist and will answer the above questions.

Here are a few purpose statements from companies to get your creative juices flowing:

Mary Kay	To give unlimited opportunity to women.
Merck	To preserve and improve human life.
3M	To solve unsolved problems innovatively.
Disney	To make people happy.

University of Texas	To transform lives through inspired learning.
Nike	To experience the emotion of competition, winning, and crushing competitors
Marriott	To make people away from home feel they are among friends and really wanted.
Wal-Mart	To give ordinary folk the chance to buy the same things as rich people.
Sony	To experience the sheer joy of advancing and applying technology for the benefit of the public.

What words capture your company's purpose?

_____

_____

_____

_____

_____

_____

Values

Much like our Core Values, our business values don't shift with trends. They act as our concrete base—sturdy and strong and unmovable!

Your values guide you through everything you do in your business, from logo design and brand development, to product or service creation, hiring, marketing campaigns, and business relationships. Your values are ever-present.

Here are some examples for a few global brands:

Adobe	Adidas	Coca-Cola
Genuine	Performance	Leadership
Exceptional	Passion	Collaboration
Innovative	Integrity	Integrity
Involved	Diversity	Accountability
		Passion
		Diversity
		Quality

Proctor & Gamble	Kellogg's	Yahoo
Integrity	Integrity	Excellence
Leadership	Accountability	Innovation
Ownership	Passion	Teamwork
Passion for Winning	A focus on success	Customer Fixation
Trust	Humility	Community
	Simplicity	Fun

As you ponder your company values, think about the characteristics that will define you in Summer and Winter as well. No matter what season you're in, your values will ground you in the *now*. They help you remain focused on what you stand for in your business and guide you in your response in any interaction or situation.

Even when you're at a Crossroads, you will turn to your personal and company values to clear the path toward your right choice.

Here is a list of some common company values:

Acceptance	Cooperation	Generosity
Accessibility	Courageous	Gratitude
Accomplish	Creative	Happiness
Accurate	Curious	Hard working
Achieve	Daring	Health
Adventure	Decisive	Helpful
Ambition	Dependable	Honesty
Appreciation	Determined	Humor
Assertiveness	Diligent	Impact
Authentic	Disciplined	Impartial
Authority	Education	Independent
Balance	Efficient	Innovative
Beauty	Empathetic	Inquisitive
Bold	Encouraging	Inspiring
Brave	Energetic	Integrity
Calm	Entrepreneur	Intelligent
Capable	Environment	Intuitive
Caring	Ethical	Justice
Challenge	Excellence	Kindness
Charitable	Fair	Knowledge
Cleanliness	Faith	Lawful
Collaborative	Family	Leadership
Community	Fearless	Learning
Compassion	Flexible	Listening
Competent	Freedom	Logical
Competitive	Friendships	Love
Connected	Fun	Loyalty

Meticulous	Practical	Self-Respect
Mindful	Prepared	Service
Nature	Private	Spirituality
Openness	Productive	Simplicity
Optimism	Realistic	Stability
Organized	Reliable	Success
Patient	Resilient	Thoughtful
Patriotic	Resourceful	Traditional
Persistent	Results-focus	Trustworthy
Philanthropy	Reputation	Truth
Play	Respect	Unique
Pleasure	Responsible	Wealth
Positive	Self-Aware	Wisdom

Now it's your time to identify a few key terms, which could expand on your personal Core Value list.

_____   _____

_____   _____

_____   _____

_____   _____

"A highly developed values system is like a compass. It serves as a guide to point you in the right direction when you are lost."

~ Idowu Koyenikan

One day in Whole Foods, I noticed the company's Core Values posted on a wall, rising fifteen feet in the air. Not only could every employee see the values every day, but every customer could as well.

When you run your business on your values, you tell everyone what you stand for, which keeps you accountable and doing business with integrity.

However, that's not always enough.

There is a difference between *having* your values list and *living* your values list. To be aligned, authentic, and in your business brilliance, you have to live your values. It's not always the easy path, but it's vital for your personal peace and business integrity.

> *"If a brand genuinely wants to make a social contribution, it should start with who they are, not what they do. For only when a brand has defined itself and its core values can it identify causes or social responsibility initiatives that are in alignment with its authentic brand story."*
> ~ **Simon Mainwaring, Author and Speaker**

Zappos, the online shoe company, is often cited as the pioneer in bringing Core Values into the culture and living them every day. Business courses at universities study Zappos and the role that its Core Values played in its rapid success. Their ten values are:

1. Deliver WOW Through Service
2. Embrace and Drive Change
3. Create Fun and A Little Weirdness
4. Be Adventurous, Creative, and Open-Minded
5. Pursue Growth and Learning
6. Build Open and Honest Relationships with Communication
7. Build a Positive Team and Family Spirit
8. Do More with Less
9. Be Passionate and Determined
10. Be Humble

This unknown company burst onto the online retail space and wow'ed customers and investors with their impressive growth and raving fan base. It didn't happen by accident, it was the way it lived its values.

Author and company sustainability expert Jim Collins spent years collecting data showing that the zealous commitment to creating strong purpose and values are the difference between companies that are built to last, and those that don't survive.

Zappos is evidence this is true.

Vision

This is where you get to imagine your brightest future, my dreamy entrepreneur friend![v]

---

v If you're in Fall or Winter, this will be really hard because you won't be able to dream about success in your business, and you won't believe you have what it takes to make it happen anyway. Revisit your Spring Cleaning strategies and bring yourself back to Summer before you create your Vision.

Your vision statement is one sentence, somewhat inspirational, painting a vivid image for your client. Describe how something will be different because of the great work your company. Here are some ideas:

Alzheimer's Association	A world without Alzheimer's disease.
Southwest Air	To become the world's most loved, most flown, most profitable airline.
IKEA	Create a better every-day life for many people.
McDonald's	To be our customers' favorite place and way to eat and drink
Feeding America	A hunger-free America.
Habitat for Humanity	A world where everyone has a decent place to live.
Microsoft (first 25 years)	A computer on every desk and in every home.
Oxfam	A just world without poverty.

Here are some tips for your process:

1. Be future-focused, capturing what you hope the world looks like because of your great business.
2. Be specific and imagine you are taking a snapshot of the future, with clarity and memorable details.

3. Use key *purpose* or *value* words that help engage readers in your hope for the future.
4. Challenge people to strive toward growth, opportunity, and making a bigger impact.

You may've noticed in the chart that Microsoft had one vision statement for twenty-five years. That's a really long time in any industry, let alone a fast-paced technology company. Within twenty-five years, it did see a computer on every desk in the developed world. Then, a few years ago, Microsoft updated its vision with the crux of it being "to help individuals and businesses realize their full potential."

Are you ready to dream about how the world will be better because of your business? Write out your preliminary vision statement here:

_____

_____

_____

_____

_____

_____

Mission

While your vision statement reflects the future, your mission statement reflects the now and the *how*.

American Diabetes Association	To prevent and cure diabetes and to improve the lives of all people affected by diabetes.
Warby Parker	To offer designer eyewear at a revolutionary price, while leading the way for socially conscious businesses.
Honest Tea	To create and promote great-tasting, healthy, organic beverages.
Cradles to Crayons	To provide children from birth through age 12, living in homeless or low-income situations, with the essential items they need to thrive—at home, at school and at play.
PBS	To create content that educates, informs and inspires.
Leukemia & Lymphoma Society	To cure leukemia, lymphoma, Hodgkin's disease and myeloma, and improve the quality of life of patients and their families.
Boy Scouts of America	To prepare young people to make ethical and moral choices over their lifetime by instilling the values of the Scout Oath and Law.

When you're thinking about your mission statement, draw inspiration from the other elements you already created: your purpose, values, and vision.

Your mission statement guides your day-to-day operations and helps you map out your route to reach your vision for your company.

Here are some other pointers:

1. Focus on who you serve, and the impact you will provide your customer, not your offerings.
2. What makes you different and unique? Weave that into your mission statement.
3. Although the level of inspiration here is lower than in your vision statement, it's important to motivate others to go on your journey with you.
4. Like the other components, make it short, sweet, real, and relevant.

_____

_____

_____

_____

_____

_____

You're in your business brilliance! Yay!

Let's look at what the four components looks like for two well-known global brands.

Company	Kellogg's Food Company
Purpose:	Nourishing families so they can flourish and thrive.
Values	Integrity, Accountability, Passion, Humility, Simplicity, Results.
Vision	To enrich and delight the world through foods and brands that matter.
Mission	We uphold our founder's dedication to people and their well-being. And we promote an environment where we can push beyond boundaries and across borders to create foods and brands that help to fuel the best in everyone everywhere.

Company	ING Financial
Purpose:	Empowering people to stay a step ahead in life and in business.
Values	Everybody needs trustworthy, determined, sensible, and accessible banks that act wise and ensure excellence in services.
Vision	To provide our customers with the most effective solutions to help them best manage their financial futures, while creating long lasting value for all stakeholders.
Mission	To be the preferred bank of our customers through operational excellence and international service quality; and of our employees with the highest level of ethical & moral values.

Now it's your turn to put it all together so you can see your magic in one magnificent place:

Company	
Purpose:	
Values	
Vision	
Mission	

Print off your glorious document so you can see it every day and really shine in your business brilliance. While we are dreamers, we are also realists, and we know the dark, Winter storms will come.

You will still be challenged.

You will still stumble, crumble, or fall.

You will still experience setbacks.

You'll wonder at the end of a long day, a long hour, or a long minute, *what's this all for? What's the point?*

Then you may collapse into your chair, sip the cold coffee you neglected for hours, and look up and see this powerful document. You'll smile and say,

"Yes, I remember. This is why I do, what I do, how I do it, and for whom I do all these things. Everything in my business has the power to impact my life, my client's lives, and the world around me."

You'll see your powerful words, feel your passion again, and will realize that these aren't just letters on a page. They have become part of the fabric of your business and who you are as a person. You can lean on them in dark and stormy times to serve as a light to help you back on your path.

> *"Successful people do all the things that unsuccessful people don't want to do."*
>
> ~ *John Paul DeJoria, Billionaire*
> *Entrepreneur of Paul Mitchell Hair Care*

CHAPTER 11

Element Four: SWOT

I *hadn't heard of the* SWOT analysis until I was a year into my business. I told a friend I was worried about a new competitor on the scene and I was afraid I would lose clients to this bold, daring woman. My friend pointed out my limiting belief: I believed there wasn't enough work for everyone. Ouch! Plus, she said, competition can make my business better, stronger, and more focused. I asked her to explain that and she taught me about SWOT.

At first, I felt I was too busy to take the time to do this work, but my anxiety and doubts only intensified. One afternoon I made some tea, ate a mountain of dark chocolate almonds, and worked on my SWOT chart. I found clarity that I hadn't felt before.

SWOT stands for:

Strengths **W**eaknesses **O**pportunities **T**hreats

Its history is a little murky, with several possible creators, but in the 1950's at Harvard, and in the 1960's at Stanford, there were several top specialists in organizational strategy studying the success or struggle of companies based on SWOT analysis.

The concept is simple. Take any industry, service, product, or even a person, and develop a more holistic view of it using a series of guided questions.

We lose our business brilliance when we're in Winter. It becomes dull, dark, lackluster, and covered in our own demoralizing negativity. Having the power to do our SWOT analysis and choose to build our businesses on our brilliance is freaking powerful!

I have seen this before so I will say it here:

Please don't weaponize your SWOT.
Please don't look at the list and see only negatives.
Please don't use this as evidence you suck.
Please don't collapse into Winter over this.

You have many strengths and opportunities. If you can't see them, check your KAST inventory list, and ask your friends, colleagues, partners, investors, or clients. You have many strengths; I know you do.

But, before we move on, I want to make some changes. I didn't like "weakness" so I looked up some synonyms and I found: *feebleness, deficiency, ineptness, shortcomings, or flaws.*

That isn't inspiring at all.

Similarly, "threat" is defined as *an intention to inflict pain injury, damage, or other hostile action.*

Yikes! Following the leadership of Carol Dweck, we're going to make these 'growth-mindset focused.'

Weaknesses   ▶   Workable Areas of Growth

Threats   ▶   Things Needing Attention

When we reframe "Workable Areas of Growth" and "Things Needing Attention," we're able to stretch, improve, and reach for success. The strength of the SWOT assessment is to provide us with information, and information is power.

Power fuels our business brilliance.

In this exercise, you may want to refer to some of your previous work, such as Core Values exploration or your KAST. *Who* you are as an entrepreneur is a big part of *what* you provide your clients. If your Core Values include dependable, honest, trustworthy, and organized, you would absolutely list these as strengths in your business SWOT.

Select a few questions from each section and take notes on your ideas and thoughts. You can select which questions you answer, and how many.

This is your SWOT!

Strengths

What is your expertise?

What do you pride yourself on in your business?

What are your competitive advantages?

What are your assets?

What personal resources do you have?

What problems do you solve really well?

Who do you have in place to help?

What is your reputation in your industry?

Do you have good systems to serve clients?

Are you a strong written/oral communicator?

Are you detail-oriented? Organized? Reliable?

Do you have unique experience/qualifications?

Do you have unique knowledge?

Do you offer great value for the price?

Do you know what you do better than others?

What is your business brilliance, your passion?

What are your technology strengths?

Are you in a network of strategic contacts?

"The sky is not my limit...I am."

~ T.F. Hodge, Author and Commentator

Workable Areas of Growth (not Weaknesses)

What are some gaps in your knowledge?

What are some negative work or personal habits?

What blocks you from delivering WOW service?

What do you avoid because you lack confidence?

What systems are not working at optimal levels?

Do you have too many projects at once?

Do you overthink options until you're stuck?

Are your perfectionist tendencies dominating?

Are you uncomfortable talking to clients?

Do you always say yes, crossing boundaries?

Are you quick to say no without thinking?

Do you try to please anyone, ideal client or not?

If money wasn't an issue, what would be better?

If time wasn't an issue, what would be better?

If energy wasn't an issue, what would be better?

If staffing wasn't an issue, what would be better?

What negative feedback have you received?

Does your business have unreliable cash flow?

> *"Never underestimate your strength. Never over-estimate your weakness."*
>
> ~ *Author Unknown*

Opportunities

Are there new markets opening up to you?

Do you have new staffing potential coming up?

Is there a more prosperous niche for you?

Do you have a new product you can create?

Do you have a new service you can offer?

Is there a business relationship you can nurture?

Have you found new ways to generate leads?

Have you met a potential collaboration partner?

Is there an unfilled need in your market/niche?

Is there a conference you can attend or speak at?

Is there a drop in shipping rates/restrictions?

Can you increase your closing rate or clients?

Is there a new cultural/fashion/lifestyle trend?

Does a competitor have a gap you can fulfill?

Have you discovered a new technology to help?

Have you had a brilliant breakthrough/idea?

Are there new advertising methods you can use?

"If you're offered a seat on a rocket ship, don't ask what seat. Just get on!"

~ Sheryl Sandberg, Strategist and Author

Things Needing Attention (not Threats)

Are your fears the biggest threat to your success?

Is there a new competitor in town?

Have you had to cut back but didn't want to?

Are there new rules/restrictions/rates coming?

Are any of your costs increasing significantly?

Are customer payments not being made?

Is there evidence of customer dissatisfaction?

Is there a decrease in demand for your offering?

Have you lost key people from your team?

Is there an increase in time for your delivery?

Is there a problem in your fulfillment systems?

Do you have rising costs in your business?

Are you doing too much and dropping things?

Do you have outdated systems or products?

Do you flip flop your offerings based on trends?

Is someone encroaching on your market?

Are there political/economic/cultural changes?

"Everything is hard before it's easy."
~ *Johann Wolfgang von Goethe, Author*

This is my SWOT.

Strengths:

_____

_____

_____

Workable Areas of Growth (not Weakness):

_____

_____

_____

Opportunities:

_____

_____

_____

Things to Pay Attention to (not Threats):

_____

_____

_____

CHAPTER 12

Element Five: Goals and Priorities

Weall have big plans and an endless to-do list that dictates how we spend our time, energy, money, and focus. Have you ever stopped to think about what gets done and what gets dropped?

Do You Set Goals?

It was March 2017. I had less than two months to do a million tasks before holding my first MamaCon conference. I was excited to welcome sixteen speakers, seventy vendors, and 150 attendees. I needed to focus.

My biggest worry was ticket sales. Part limiting belief, part truth, I was afraid women were too tired and didn't want one more thing on their plate. But I knew if they saw this as a break and not another burden, they would happily sign up. How could I reach all the moms who would benefit from coming?

I looked at my calendar; I had fifty-one days until we came together in a day of education, inspiration, and celebration. How could I spread the word about this amazing day? I needed bold, brave action.

That afternoon, I spontaneously posted a video on Facebook offering to help fifty women do anything they needed for one hour a day for the next fifty days. I thought if ten women contacted me to receive an hour of service and support, they might come to MamaCon. Right away, I wanted to delete it, I mean, who did I think I was to put myself out there? (Hello, Winter) I left it up and went inside to make dinner.

Requests poured in right away and didn't stop for weeks. Over the next month, the video was viewed 5000 times. A local newspaper ran an article on it, and I was asked to speak about my '50 Mamas in 50 Days' Campaign on local television. By the day of my event, I'd helped fifty-nine women garden, declutter, meal-plan, cook, brainstorm businesses, set goals, create chore charts, and create self-care practices. I helped fifty-nine women find a spark of hope, joy, laughter, calmness, and connection. I had potentially impacted the lives of fifty-seven spouses, 138 children, and countless others I will never know about. All while planning MamaCon. And being a mom and wife. Did I sell more tickets? I have no idea. I didn't even mention my event to them, but the buzz helped me a lot.

Was it hard? Yes.

Was it worth it? Absolutely.

Would I have been so successful if I had said, "If you need help, let me know,"? Absolutely not. It rocked because I said, 'fifty women, fifty days, anything you need for an hour.' That's the power of setting a goal.

> *"Would you tell me, please, which way I ought to go from here?' 'That depends a good deal on where you want to get to,' said the Cat. 'I don't much care where--' said Alice. 'Then it doesn't matter which way you go,' said the Cat."*
>
> *~ from "Alice in Wonderland"*
> *by Lewis Carroll*

Why Set Goals?

Goals are incredibly effective to find momentum for our Purpose, Values, Vision and Mission, while capitalizing on the strengths in our businesses. When we set goals, we choose what's most important, what creates the best returns, and how we spend our resources, time, money, and energy.

Creating goals also provides the opportunity to dream. Setting goals, both big and small, shifts us into a proactive, growth-focused mindset and lets us twist the kaleidoscope to see things in a brand new way.

Truthfully, setting great goals takes you off auto-pilot and gets you moving toward your desired result.

Research shows that the act of planning is the single best technique to reduce stress.

If the idea of setting goals sounds overwhelming, don't worry—you already do it without knowing.

- You set targets for revenue, sales, or customers
- You set aside money to buy courses you want
- You check out who will be attending the same event as you so you can connect with them

Building a business takes time, but time is often a huge source of stress for entrepreneurs. On any given day, we stress because we just don't have enough time. But when we look at the business landscape, the true equalizer *is* time—we all have the same amount. How you use your time is where the difference lies.

Dr. Gail Matthews, a psychology professor at the Dominican University in California, recently studied the art and science of goal setting. She surveyed 267 people and split them into two groups: those who wrote down their goals and dreams, and those who didn't. She found we're 42% more likely to achieve our goals by writing them down on a regular basis. That number goes up if you have a goal, write it down, and share with someone who believes in you.

If goals are so powerful, and they are so empowering, why don't we set them all the time?

Most people want to achieve their goals, but either don't have the systems in place to meet their goals, or don't know what it actually takes to get there.

When we take care of the first issue, the second will solve itself. You'll need grit and commitment. But you have those things already because you're an entrepreneur with business brilliance!

So, let's check in.

How many business goals are you working on right now? It's okay if you have two, one, or even none! We're here to dive into goal setting together.

As we learned in previous chapters, our brains are powerful enough to take our thoughts, beliefs, and values and manifest them in our lives. If we spend time listening to our Automatic Negative Thoughts (ANTs), we'll feel trapped and consumed by our Winter stories.

When we use time dreaming, planning and taking bold action, we move in the direction of our dreams.

There are many goal-setting books, programs, and apps you can choose from, but I like to keep it simple. If you've never set any business goals before, this can be overwhelming. I encourage you to take what you need and leave the rest for another time.

The first step is to answer: in what area of my business would I like to set a goal?

One thing to keep in mind is something called the 80/20 Rule, or the Pareto Principle. This rule says that 80% of our results comes from 20% of our work.

When it comes to sales, Pareto would claim 80% of our sales come from 20% of our clients. In business development, Pareto would say 80% of our contracts come from 20% of our relationships, and so on.

As you're deciding on your goal, determine what 20% brings in 80% of your business results. Invest your time, energy, and resources there.

Yoga expert and entrepreneur Saraya wanted to buy new equipment for her studio, and she wanted to earn the money instead of dipping into her savings. We looked at her numbers and she was shocked to learn that 80% of her income came from private yoga clients, not from her weekly classes or online membership group.

With this new knowledge, she set a goal to earn $2000 in a month by only offering more private yoga coaching sessions. That's a good start, but not a good goal because experts in goal-setting say there are regular goals—which are simple, open-to-interpretation, and often ineffective—and then there are S.M.A.R.T. goals.

The S.M.A.R.T. Goal Setting System

When we set a regular goal in business, it can be hit-or-miss if it happens. But when we set a S.M.A.R.T. goal, very little can stand in our way. Having a clearly defined, specific outcome is key here. The S.M.A.R.T. method move you from goal-set to goal-success.

The basic premise requires goals to be:

S – Specific (Who, what, where, when, why?)
M – Measurable (How to know it's reached?)
A – Achievable (Can we accomplish this goal?)
R – Relevant (Is it aligned with all our goals?)
T – Timely (When will it be completed?)

Let's consider Saraya's goal again.
Earn $2000 a month from private yoga coaching.

Now let's put that through the S.M.A.R.T. system:

During April, I'll hold a flash sale at $62.50 per session for my private yoga coaching. I'll schedule four new Tuesday and four new Thursday sessions.

Specific: 4 Tue./4 Thurs. sessions, $62.50 per session.
Measurable: Increase in bookings and income.
Achievable: I have a waitlist, so I'm sure I'll fill up.
Relevant: Builds my expertise in my business.
Timely: It's only for the month of April.

Saraya admitted her previous goals were rarely achieved because they were too vague, but this new system allowed her to make super clear goals, buy her new equipment, double her client load, and increase client satisfaction because their sessions were more advanced with this new equipment.

How do you create your business goals?

Some people already have a great goal-setting system and that's awesome! For those who would like a bit more support, we'll explore a step-by-step way you can create a business goal that supports your brilliance and brings you to Summer!

How to Create a Business Goal:

Step 1: Brainstorm all ideas for goals

Step 2: Sort your ideas into categories

Step 3: Rank ideas in each category (best first)

Step 4: Select ONE goal

Step 5: Brainstorm your action list

Step 6: Order your action list on your Goal Sheet

Step 7: Identify obstacles and solutions

Step 8: List resources

Step 9: Select milestones

Step 10: Set a timeline

Step 11: Make sure it's S.M.A.R.T.

Step 12: Execute on the plan

Step 13: Track and analyze

Step 14: Course correct if necessary

Step 15: Celebrate when you reach your goal!

Step 1: Brainstorm All Ideas for Goals
Write down every idea on paper, there are no right or wrong ideas. How do you like to brainstorm?

List Makers
These people live and breathe lists and make them with joy and ease. They tend to think in sequential order, preferring traditionally organized material.

Mind Mappers
These people see patterns, shapes, and relationships. They start in the center with a key idea, and then write every thought around the key idea.

Sticky Noters
These people want the freedom and flexibility to move ideas around to find order or sequence. Multi-color papers bring them joy.

Step 2: Sort Your Ideas into Categories

No matter what system you use to brainstorm, after twenty or so ideas, you will see that they belong to different parts of your business, such as sales, legal, marketing, product development, finance, billing, client acquisition, technology, content creation, etc.

You can make as many categories as you need to accurately represent the full scope of your business.

Step 3: Rank Ideas in Each Category (Best first)

Under each category, organize your ideas in order of importance (based on your definition of success, your values, client needs, etc.). Since we're in business to support our dreams and receive money for helping others solve their struggles, keep an eye on your return on investment (ROI) when ordering the ideas in each category. Rank them so the items that bring in the highest revenue for the least output are at the top.

Step 4: Select ONE Goal

It might be a bit intoxicating to have all these great ideas sitting there, waiting for you to bring them to life! Dear friend, let's go slow. At this point you may have many categories with some possible goals listed, or a few categories with many goals.

Select the top goal in one category to set as your goal to work on first. This goal should support your Purpose, Values, Vision, and Mission, and moves your business forward toward your dream destination.

Step 5: Brainstorm an Action List
Yay! You have selected one goal you want to focus on to bring the biggest win to your business. Now, brainstorm again, but this time write out every single action you must do to reach that one goal. If you have a small goal, you might have five action items listed but a larger goal might need thirty action items.

Step 6: Order Your Action List on Your Goal Sheet
List all action items in chronological or sequential order. (First do this, then this, then that)

Step 7: Identify Obstacles and Solutions
We won't know all the obstacles we might face, but we can list things we expect to encounter.

For example, if one of your action steps is "Collect payments," an obstacle is "payment may be late." (And, make a note to study *why* we tolerate late payments.)

Beside each obstacle, write how you can actively manage that obstacle, such as "send an early reminder about payment due," or, "add a late fine to contract."

Step 8: List Resources
Even if you feel stuck, you're more resource-rich than you think! Think about people you know, online resources or groups, specialists or referrals, products/ apps you could buy, workshops you could take.

Step 9: Select milestones

Milestones are checkpoints to see if you're on track to meet your goal. They serve to confirm if all things continue at this pace, you will be successful.

For example, if your goal is to secure two new clients, and your method of client acquisition includes mailing out postcards, a milestone could be sending out 100 postcards each Monday for three weeks.

Step 10: Set Timeline

Some goals are short-term, some are long-term.

Pick a short-term goal first so you can go through the process quickly, testing it out in your business before selecting a long-term goal.

When it's time to set your timeline, look closely at your calendar, holidays, and non-negotiable items. Block off enough time to meet the goal. You don't want to unleash your ANTs by thinking you can't do it when really you underestimated how long it would take you.

Step 11: Make Sure it's S.M.A.R.T.

These goals need the S.M.A.R.T. treatment:

S – Specific (Who, what, where, when, why?)

M – Measurable (How to know it's reached?)

A – Achievable (Can we accomplish this goal?)

R – Relevant (Is it aligned with all our goals?)

T – Timely (When will this goal be completed?)

Step 12: Execute on the Plan

Nike was right... just do it! This is head-down, diligently moving toward your goal in full focus-mode.

Step 13: Track and Analyze

Regularly review your progress, update your action steps, adjust the timeline, and check on your measurable items. For example, did you send out 100 postcards every Monday for three weeks?

Step 14: Course Correct If Necessary

If you noticed something was off-track, investigate that in a deeper way. Are you not meeting targets with postcard mailing because you don't have enough addresses? Or ran out of stamps?

If your goal has a soft end date, which means it doesn't have a set launch date, adjust your timeline. If your dates are set, you can remove some of the nice-to-have action items and save them for 'Version 2.0.'

Step 15: Celebrate When You Reach Your Goal!

Wow! There may have been a few days when you doubted you could do but here you are! You did it!

You made decisions and choices along the way to support your dream of moving your business forward. Congratulations, my friend!

Now, celebrate your win, however big or small, and make a habit of enjoying the Summer feeling of doing something awesome for your business growth.

Priorities

Let's be real. There's never enough of us to go around. As busy entrepreneurs, we choose over and over what gets our attention and energy. It's normal in Fall times to pick the low-hanging fruit or grease the squeaky wheel, but we need to set our priorities based on our Core Values, Purpose, Values, Vision, Mission and Goals to really connect to our business brilliance.

While goals and priorities are often interchanged, they aren't the same: a goal is something you set for your future, a priority is what you do daily or weekly to stay on the right path toward your goal.

Important vs. Not Important

In the rush of life, it's easy to jump into reaction mode, which to be honest, is a pathway to Winter. We scramble to take on every single thing as it pops up. We focus intently on that until the next thing pops up.

Your Summer self who is capable, confident, and powerful can get lost in the whirlwind of unfinished tasks. Your inner critic might see your lack of being able to manage *all-the-things* as proof of failure. In all reality, it's your system that's failing you.

What's on your list that is *truly* important?

Let's just not *think* about our to-do list, let's *see* it.

Write down all of the tasks currently on your 'Today/ This Week' List (I know it's LONG!)

_____   _____

_____   _____

_____   _____

If you're like me, your list has (some) important and (too many) unimportant tasks. When we're juggling too many things, we put ourselves in the path of the perfect storm and risk falling into a Winter cycle of negativity, can't-do-it-ness/not-enoughness. Maybe you begin reciting your perfected monologue entitled, *101 Reasons I'm a Crappy Entrepreneur.*

When you're o-v-e-r-l-o-a-d-e-d, you open the door for disconnection, defensive or destructive responses, reactivity, negativity, all-or-nothing thinking, or the blaming/shaming cycle to bring in intense storms, pushing you back into Winter.

What Have You Been Prioritizing Lately?

What on your list is *truly* important?

What needs to be done today? This week?

What can wait a few weeks? A month?

What is busywork, not goal-achieving work?

Spend a few moments and go through your to-do list with the courage to remove all unnecessary tasks. Be ruthless. Once you've streamlined and decluttered your list, we'll intentionally prioritize the people, commitments, and business goals we value the most.

We want to be in business brilliance and spend time in the beautiful, connected days of Summer, but dreaming isn't doing. If we say our strong mindset and our successful business are our highest priorities, we need to reflect that in how we spend our time. We juggle hundreds of things each week, so to have the time and energy to pursue our best life, we must only do important, necessary things.

Your priorities are a roadmap for your life. They illuminate the path to your goal at the end of the road. When you have your priorities ranked from most important to least important, it's easy to make decisions or say yes (or no) to new commitments. Your map will tell you if your decision will keep you moving toward your goal, or off into the weeds.

> *"Things which matter most must never be at the*
> *mercy of things which matter least."*
> ~ **Johann Wolfgang von Goethe, Author**

People often say, "This sounds great, but I have no time." Or, "If you knew how busy I was, you'd cry."

I get it, I've been there: running as fast as you can, stopping when you drop. Is that how you want to live?

No one ever says, "Yes! Frenetic-living-hamster-wheeling is my dream life." So let's fix that.

The Eisenhower Decision Matrix

Most of us know this tool, even if the name is unfamiliar. When we list out everything on our list, we can categorize them all into one of four quadrants:

	Urgent	Not Urgent
Important	(do these first)	(schedule these soon so they don't become urgent)
Not Important	(delegate or batch process these to get them done)	(delete these)

Using this matrix removes the guesswork. If you have two extra hours this week to work, do you attend the general networking meeting, or do you prepare your presentation for the Chamber of Commerce meeting? Using the matrix, there is no guessing.

If you have clear goals, you're ready to set your priorities. However, if you're in between projects, or at a Crossroads where you're not sure what to build, this next activity will help you the most.

Wish Week

Imagine for a moment that you open your planner and look at your Wish Week.

What do you see?

Does your planner list things that bring you joy?

Are you working on things you're passionate about, in ways that help make the world a better place?

What does your Monday look like?

Your Tuesday?

Every other day?

What time would your day start?

When would it end?

Use the next calendar to create what you WISH your week would look like right now. Not your dream life from the Future Me exercise earlier in the book. Your very best life in your current situation. Include what you wish your current week was filled with, like:

Ideal Week as an Entrepreneur

	Sun	Mon	Tues	Wed	Thu	Fri	Sat
6am							
7am							
8am							
9am							
10am							
11am							
12pm							
1pm							
2pm							
3pm							
4pm							
5pm							
6pm							
7pm							
8pm							
9pm							
10pm							

Look at all the awesome ways you're living the life of your dreams! You're prioritizing your treasured activities, relationships, and joys, dedicating quality time on business growth using your KAST. Nice!

- Events
- Activities
- Commitments
- Appointments
- Client Time

- CEO time
- Family time
- Creative time
- Self-care time

I hate to burst the bubble of happiness right now, but we need to put our Wish Week aside for a moment.

Let's do this exercise again using *our actual week in our actual life*. Include all the time you work on your business and client work, plus family time, hobbies, self-care, errands, volunteering, cooking, cleaning, browsing social media and binge-watching shows.

> *"Time is free, but priceless. You can't own it, but you can use it. You can't keep it, but you can spend it. Once you've lost it you can never get it back."*
>
> *~ Harvey Mackay,*
> *7-time NYT Bestselling Author*

Actual Week from your current life

	Sun	Mon	Tues	Wed	Thu	Fri	Sat
6am							
7am							
8am							
9am							
10am							
11am							
12pm							
1pm							
2pm							
3pm							
4pm							
5pm							
6pm							
7pm							
8pm							
9pm							
10pm							

It may be tempting to leave off the time you spend wandering the aisles of Target, or walking the dog or volunteering at your child's school, but you need to list everything so you know what you're currently prioritizing, and what you need to add or remove to get closer to your Wish Week schedule.

For my creative friends, you can color code for visual organization so you can see very clearly where you spend your time. Don't forget to make a legend so you know what each color means! Here's an example:

Green: Self-care: health and wellness appointments, baths, reading, exercising, meditation, journaling

Yellow: (whoever is the sunshine of your life!) Meaningful/fun time with spouse, kids, pets.

Red: Everything business, such as client work, sales, meetings, website/marketing/social media.

Orange: Writing, research, anything related to books, reading, learning, or self-discovery.

Purple: Being in Mom-mode. Chauffeuring, homework help, watching their activities, their appointments.

Blue: Being in Helper-mode. Volunteering, calling friends, helping out with schools/sports

Pink: Home life day-to-day. Cooking, cleaning, laundry, shopping, pet care, car maintenance, gardening.

Brown: Home life management. Insurance, banking, bills, renovations, research travel plans, repairs.

Are you shocked at how you spend your time? I was! When I color-coded my Actual Week, I saw I spent more time than I realized in some categories (driving, being a helper) and less time in other categories (self-care, not enough fun with my kids).

Color-coded or not, once you look at your calendar, you will see extraordinary demands on your time. I honor you for how hard you work in your life. You carry a lot on your shoulders!

Remember our Wish Week? That's our ideal calendar, how we would love to organize our time. We may not get there 100% today, but we'll begin. First, slash things you don't want. Make room for growth, connection, and attention on our business.

Rip out your weeds, folks, and remove the absurd amount of stressful activities we manage every day. It puts us at risk for a possible slide back into Winter because we're stretched too thin.

With your Actual Week calendar, what can you:

- Accelerate (Cut dilly-dallying, get it done)
- Automate (Auto-pay, order products online)
- Consolidate (Batch things together)
- Delegate (Give it to someone else to do)
- Eliminate (Decide it isn't important)

Now the fun begins!

On the next page, you'll find a new calendar called *Your Week Redefined*, and it will help you blend items from your Wish Week with urgent/important items from your Actual Week. This is where your intentions and goals meet your time and resources.

As you go through this process, decide if each item is worthy of your time. Does this align with my goals? Does it honor my Purpose, Values, Vision and Mission?

Your time is valuable. It's actually the most precious thing you have. Protect it fiercely!

"Where focus goes, energy flows."
~ Anthony Robbins, Motivational Speaker

One thing to note is *when* should you schedule an task in your day? Consider your energy, productive/ non-productive times, and family needs.

Without question, though, I recommend, as best as possible, putting your harder, more demanding tasks earlier in the day and earlier in the week when you're rested and ready to go. Adding a difficult task on a Friday afternoon is just asking for your ANTs to flood you with feelings of failure, shoving you into Winter.

Once you have filled out your schedule, you can feel confident that you're living in alignment with your heart's desires. As entrepreneurs, we can get lost in the weeds, working endlessly and tirelessly, but then we lose sight of what we're trying to do in the world and who we're doing it for.

With this calendar, you can be confident knowing you're moving toward your dreams, while honoring the awesome, brilliant business owner you are!

"The question I ask myself like almost every day is, 'Am I doing the most important thing I could be doing?'"
~ Mark Zuckerberg, CEO Facebook

Step 1: add your non-negotiables/must-do tasks.

Step 2: add time for self-care because you matter.

Step 3: add in time with partner, children, pets.

Step 4: add time to work on/in your business.

Step 6: add work time for networking, meetings, etc.

Step 7: add in homelife chores, responsibilities.

Step 8: add in other 'nice-to-have' items.

Your Week Redefined

	Sun	Mon	Tues	Wed	Thu	Fri	Sat
6am							
6:30							
7am							
7:30							
8am							
8:30							
9am							
9:30							
10am							
10:30							
11am							
11:30							
12pm							
12:30							
1pm							
1:30							
2pm							
2:30							
3pm							
3:30							
4pm							
4:30							
5pm							
5:30							
6pm							
6:30							
7pm							
7:30							
8pm							
8:30							
9pm							

CHAPTER 13

Using The Five Elements

On our journey through the Five Elements of Awareness, we covered a lot of ground:

We discovered what KAST we have in our hot little hands right now. We acknowledged skills and abilities we often discount and accepted our brilliance.

We identified our Core Values that consciously and unconsciously shape our perspective. We realized we have specific Core Values from our family of origin and our experiences, yet we can be intentional to choose Core Values that help us as entrepreneurs.

We explored our Purpose, Values, Vision, and Mission statements which will guide our business strategies, decisions, and goals. These principles provide us with the confidence to know who we are, where we'll go, what we focus on, and how to invest our time, money, and energy.

We learned about our SWOT, our strengths and areas of growth required to be the level of entrepreneur we'd like to be. We brainstormed some new opportunities for growing our businesses.

We learned how to create a step-by-step plan to set effective business goals and how to use those goals to define our true priorities. When we remove 'busyness,' we elevate people, projects, and dreams that matter most so we live in our purpose.

When we schedule all the important items into our calendars, they'll happen.

This extensive collection of entrepreneur-exploration tools and systems will catapult you from many Winter days to mostly Summer days.

Why?

When you know yourself, your strengths, talents, and gifts, when you're confident the foundation of your business is solid, and when you have identified struggling areas, you can create a plan to overcome those challenges. Now, there is no storm big enough to take away your business brilliance!

There's one more flower I want to plant in your entrepreneurial garden before we part ways.

CHAPTER 14

Growing Together

MY DAD WAS A SAILOR FROM NEWFOUNDLAND.

*A*s *a young man,* he often sailed off the coast of eastern Canada in the unpredictable Atlantic waters. He saw how dangerous the ocean could be and he developed a deep respect and love for lighthouses. He knew in every dark, stormy night, the flicker from a lighthouse was all a crew needed to right the course.

I urge you: look for the lighthouses in your life.

Of course, this book is your forever reference. You can also find info great online (websites, podcasts, videos) or ask your fellow entrepreneurs to assist you. All of these can be a lighthouse for you.

But, these are all *external* options. Your first move is always to turn inward. Search your heart. Ask your higher power to illuminate your next best step. In both our glorious, sweet Summer and in our bleak, blustery Winter, we aren't always making giant leaps. Often, we move forward one itty-bitty step at a time, and most days we just need a flicker of light to guide us.

Final Thoughts

Now that you've experienced the power and possibility of mastering your mindset to celebrate your business brilliance, you have limitless potential for happiness and prosperity. You know who you are.

Your top goal every day is to be the best version of you for yourself, your family, and your business.

You will experience every season, that is a fact. However, every time you reach the Crossroads, know that you have all of your experience, intuition, and wisdom to guide you. If you wobble or feel a little ungrounded, return to these practices:

- Commit to honoring your purpose, values, vision and mission and stay true to your principles.
- Honor your greatness. If you falter, use your KAST list for the depth, breadth, and extent of your gifts.
- Revisit your goals and priorities. If they're too big, break them down further to be successful.
- Journal about your thoughts and feelings. Keep challenging your fears, doubts, and beliefs.
- Build meaningful self-care practices.
- Read everything to go deeper into self-awareness.
- Share your experiences with amazing friends who also follow *The 5 Seasons of Connection* philosophy.
- Find *The 5 Seasons Life* on social media. Join our community to find encouragement, inspiration, and actionable strategies to live your best life.

The purpose of *The 5 Seasons* is to help you know the seasons of your mindset, recognize when you're slipping into the chilliness of Fall or the dark days of Winter, build a bridge back to Spring, and celebrate the glow of Summer in all your business brilliance. At the Crossroads, you learn you have the power.

You get to choose.

When we learn how to weather the storms on our business journey and guide ourselves back to that safe, happy place, we'll enjoy all the beauty of the season.

Keep in mind that everyday won't be big sales and business wins. There'll be days when we can only meet the basic needs of our business because we're running on fumes. Practice self-care, read your Manifesto and KAST list, and give yourself grace to rest and recharge.

In my hundreds of business decisions every week, I don't always get it right and I've practiced these strategies countless times! Be gentle with yourself. Take more time at the Crossroads if you need it. Stay there all day if you need to.

Trust yourself.

You're more ready than you think.

Entrepreneurialism is never perfect, but it's a magnificent, spirited, profoundly personal journey.

My hope is that armed with this new model for self-awareness, you'll feel more confident facing each day in your business. You have a massive collection of evidence of your talents, skills, knowledge, passion, and abilities. When Winter comes, or the ANTs show up at your picnic, you will know exactly how to walk away and go toward your Summer-self. Now that we've explored The 5 Seasons, you'll feel connected to your purpose and your business in ways you've never experienced before, and the world will be a better place because you'll shine even brighter. I can't wait to see you show up authentically, fiercely, confidently, unapologetically, boldly, bravely, brilliantly you! (Please find me online and share with me your story – I'd love to hear how The 5 Seasons has impacted your life and your business!)

Thank you for inviting me into your life and your business; I hope I've served as a lighthouse for your journey. On your stormiest nights, I pray *The 5 Seasons of Connection* will help you find your way so you can enjoy long, beautiful Summer days.

Now, go share your brilliance!

> *"Go confidently in the direction of your dreams.*
> *Live the life you have imagined."*
>
> ~ **Henry David Thoreau,**
> **Philosopher and Poet**

Gratitudes

I'm grateful for you, my brave new friend. I hope you found value here for your business and life. Keep connecting to your brilliance, in every possible way!

I'm grateful for my sister, Dorothy. She has been the greatest sister CEO I could ever have: encouraging me to carry on, to dig a little deeper, and share a little more. She is my lighthouse and in every storm, she's there for me.

I'm grateful for my mom, Isabelle, and brother, David. And my dad, who is playing Newfie songs in heaven for me.

I'm grateful for Katie Cross, my editor, who graciously agreed to work with me again. Your genius is limitless!

I'm grateful for Christy Keating, my phenomenal accountability partner and heartful friend. I adore you!

I'm grateful for my Seattle-area biz sisters in BAM, Girlfriend's Success Circle, and Illuminating Women who encouraged me to reach for the farthest star and hold tight.

I'm grateful to the friendships and support I've found in Biz Chix and the FB group, Coffee With Dan, especially Amanda Leek, who connected with me heart to heart and gifted me with her business brilliance.

I'm grateful to my clients who brought The 5 Seasons into their businesses to great success. I burst with joy!

Finally, I'm so grateful for my family. Jack, thank you for your love and support while I found the seasons and brought them to life. I'm so very thankful for you!

Without question, my best and brightest Summer days are those spent with my three kids. There's no scale to measure how deeply and entirely I love and cherish Alex, Nicole, and Michael. I am profoundly blessed and eternally honored to be their mom. Thank you for choosing me :)

Sweeties, may your lives be long Summer days filled with love, laughter, and light, but remember when the storms come, you know what to do. Trust your heart.

I am, and forever will be, a lighthouse for your journey. I love you endlessly!

Endnotes

1. Edwards, Martha. "16 celebrity quotes on suffering with impostor syndrome." *Marie Claire,* Nov 11, 2016. https://www.marieclaire.co.uk/entertainment/celebrity-quotes-on-impostor-syndrome-434739#skYCWcMFSlXAPdik.99

2. Simon, Phil. "The Empress Has No Clothes: An Interview with Joyce Roche." Huffington Post, July 15, 2013. https://www.huffingtonpost.com/phil-simon/the-empress-has-no-clothe_b_3601497.html

3. "Crossroads | Definition of Crossroads in English by Oxford Dictionaries." *Oxford Dictionaries* Oxford Dictionaries, oxforddictionaries.com/definition/crossroads.

4. Lieberman, Matthew. The social brain and its superpowers. TEDx St. Louis Oct 7, 2013. https://www.youtube.com/watch?v=NNhk3owF7RQ

5. Earley PhD, Jay. Inner Critic Types. https://personal-growth-programs.com/inner-critic-section/inner-critic-types/

6. Amen, Daniel Dr. Gain Control Over Negative Self-Talk. Amen Clinic Website, November 5, 2013. https://www.amenclinics.com/blog/gain-control-over-negative-self-talk/

7. Lewis, Becky. The Root Causes of Anger that Could Be Hiding in Your Subconscious. Learning Mind, September 13th, 2018. https://www.learning-mind.com/causes-of-anger/

8. Sakulku, Jaruwan, James Alexander. "The Impostor Phenomenon." International Journal of Behavioral Science, Vol 6, No.1. 2011. https://www.tci-thaijo.org/ index.php/IJBS/article/view/521/pdf

9. Cuddy, Amy. I Don't Deserve to be Here: Presence and the Impostor Syndrome. Lean In. March 3, 2016. https://leanin.org/news-inspiration/overcoming-imposter-syndrome-to-reveal-your-presence

10. Briggs, Saga. "25 Ways to Develop a Growth Mindset." InformED. February 10, 2015. https://www.opencolleges.edu.au/informed/features/develop-a-growth-mindset/

11. Gross-Loh, Christine. "How Praise Became a Consolation Prize." The Atlantic, December 16, 2016. https://www.theatlantic.com/education/archive/2016/12/ how-praise-became-a-consolation-prize/510845/

12. Nagel, Jackie. "Gratitude's 10 Proven Results on Business Growth." Huffington Post, December 6, 2017. https://www.huffingtonpost.com/jackie-nagel/gratitudes-10-proven-resu_b_8711232.html

13. "Forgiveness Definition | What Is Forgiveness." *Greater Good*, greatergood. berkeley.edu/topic/forgiveness/definition.
14. "10 Benefits of Forgiveness." Purpose Beyond Pain, 2010. https://purpose beyondpain.wordpress.com/2010/02/08/10-benefits-of-forgiveness/
15. Kim, W.Chan and Renée Mauborgne. What is Blue Ocean Shift? 2017. https://www.blueoceanstrategy.com/what-is-blue-ocean-shift/
16. Knight, Craig and S. Alexander Haslam. Relative Merits of Lean, Enriched and Empowered Offices. University of Exeter Journal of Experimental Psychology: Applied. February 8, 2010 https://www.identityrealization.com/app/download/ 5783859520/2010+JEP+Space+Experiments.pdf
17. Kappel, Mike. "What's the One Task Most Small-Business Owners Loathe?" Entrepreneur.com. Jan. 28, 2015. https://www.entrepreneur.com/article/240875
18. Fortune 500 Rank. Fortune. http://fortune.com/fortune500/avon-products/
19. Burgstone, Jon and Bill Murphy Jr. "Why Entrepreneurs Do What They Do." Inc. February 15, 2012. https://www.inc.com/jon-burgstone/why-god-loves-entrepreneurs.html
20. Happiness. Psychology Today. https://www.psychologytoday.com/us/basics/happiness
21. "What is the Science of Happiness?" Berkeley Wellness, November 2015. http://www.berkeleywellness.com/healthy-mind/mind-body/article/what-science-happiness
22. Steptoe, Andrew and Jane Wardle. "Positive Affect and Biological Function in Everyday Life." Science Direct, December 2005. https:// www.sciencedirect.com/science/article/pii/S0197458005002769
23. Davidson, Karina W, Elizabeth Mostofsky and William Whang. "Don't worry, be happy: positive affect and reduced 10-year incident coronary heart disease." National Center for Biotechnology Information, Feb 17, 2010. https://www.ncbi.nlm.nih.gov/pmc/articles/ PMC2862179/
24. Marsland, Anna L. SheldonCohen, Bruce S.Rabin, Stephen B.Manuck. "Trait positive affect and antibody response to hepatitis B vaccination." Science Direct, May 2006. https://www.sciencedirect.com/science/article/pii/S088915910500139X
25. Zautra, Alez J. PhD, Lisa M. Johnson MA, Mary C. Davis PhD. "Positive Affect as a Source of Resilience for Women in Chronic Pain." National Center for Biotechnology Information, April 7, 2005. https://www.ncbi.nlm.nih.gov/pmc/articles/PMC2593933/

26. Lyubomirsky, Sonja. *The How of Happiness: a Scientific Approach to Getting the Life You Want.* Penguin Press, 2008.

27. Transferable Skills Inventory. UC Davis Internship and Career Center. July 29, 2015. https://icc.ucdavis.edu/sites/g/files/dgvnsk2236/files/local_resources/ handouts/transferable-skills-inventory.pdf

28. Collins, Jim. Vision Framework 2001. https://www.jimcollins.com/tools/vision-framework.pdf

29. R, Heryati. 190 Brilliant Examples of Company Values https://inside.6q.io/190-examples-of-company-values/

30. Collins, Jim. Building Companies to Last. 1995. https://www.jimcollins.com/article_topics/articles/building-companies.html

31. Kellogg Company Vision and Purpose. https://www.kelloggcompany.com/en_US/our-vision-purpose.html. Also see https://hbr.org/2014/09/your-companys-purpose-is-not-its-vision-mission-or-values

32. ING Bank Vision, Mission and Values. https://www.ingbank.com.tr/en/ingbank/corporate-governance/our-vision-mission-and-values Also see https:// hbr.org/ 2014/09/your-companys-purpose-is-not-its-vision-mission-or-values

33. http://healthland.time.com/2011/05/31/study-25-of-happiness-depends-on-stress-management/

34. Morrissey, Mary. The Power of Writing Down Your Goals and Dreams. Huffington Post. Dec 06, 2017 https://www.huffingtonpost.com/marymorrissey/the-power-of-writing-down_b_12002348.html

Join the conversation about harnessing
the power of Your Business Brilliance!

Connect with me online at:

www.5SeasonsLife.com

hello@5SeasonsLife.com

www.facebook.com/groups/5SeasonsLife/

www.linkedin.com/in/leannekabat/

www.instagram.com/5seasonslife/

To deepen your connection to your children,
pick up the books that started it all!

Available now on Amazon

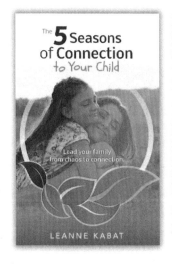 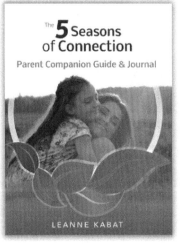